SpringerBriefs in Economics

For further volumes:
http://www.springer.com/series/8876

Gagari Chakrabarti · Chitrakalpa Sen

Anatomy of Global Stock Market Crashes

An Empirical Analysis

Springer

Gagari Chakrabarti
Economics
Presidency University
College Street 86/1
Kolkata 700 073
West Bengal
India

Chitrakalpa Sen
G D Goenka Education City
Department of Economics
G D Goenka World Institute
Sohna-Gurgaon Road
Gurgaon 122103
India

ISSN 2191-5504 e-ISSN 2191-5512
ISBN 978-81-322-0462-6 e-ISBN 978-81-322-0463-3
DOI 10.1007/978-81-322-0463-3
Springer New Delhi Heidelberg New York Dordrecht London

Library of Congress Control Number: 2011944258

Printed on acid-free paper

Springer is part of Springer Science+Business Media (www.springer.com)

Foreword

Despite recurrent shocks to the stock market, a disastrous association of stock market with the real sector is required to turn our attention to its importance. After the great depression of the 1930s, it is the current financial sector crisis including the stock market crash that has particularly caught our attention. Only, this time, the severity and extent of the crash and its effect is deeper and wider since now both financial and real sector, courtesy globalization and technological innovation, stands globally integrated.

It is said that value and movements of stock market is ultimately determined by the real sector. It has also been expressed in the current historical juncture of capitalism that financial sector in general and stock sector in particular exercise considerable control over the real sector. Perhaps, both are true. Not surprisingly then and despite the dispute which is the primary causal factor, stock market shifts and real sectors shifts tend to move concomitantly, positively during the time of boom and negatively during the bust with each feeding into the other.

Notwithstanding this state of affairs, much research has also gone into the endogenous factors that generate dynamics within the stock market independent of the real sector. Thus it is conjectured that there may be events transpiring in the stock market that may make it implode from within. Boom and bubble may thus have to do with events that happen in the stock markets which, given the technological transformation of the last two decades, generates speedy decisions–actions that are not only unpredictable, but may also be what are called irrational leading to a path dependent trajectory where the herd mentality of following others take precedence over the rationally calculating decision of cost-benefit. The result is a non-linear, chaotic, stock market with self-generating fluctuations and indeterminate equilibrium. If the current history of capitalism is about the financial control of stock market, then this endogenously produced cycles bordering on unpredictability and contingency in the stock market only reiterates the unstable nature of the capitalist system per se. Moreover, are all of the phases of boom and bubble unique or are there some common factors, such as rising/eroding confidence that are linked with the various cyclic phases?

Distilling the frontier of the debates on these issues, Gagari Chakrabarti and Chitrakalpa Sen produce a fascinating analysis of the history and cause of the cycles of stock market, with particular attention to the current global crisis. It will help the reader understand the current nuances of stock markets, its dynamics of booms and busts and, why, even if we may know about the factor of confidence, the trajectory of cycles may lead to indeterminate outcomes. This book is a must read for those interested in the role of stock market in the current global economic crisis.

Kolkata, October 2011

Anjan Chakrabarti
Department of Economics
University of Calcutta
Kolkata
India

Preface

September 15, 2008 did not start as just another day in our lives. The world woke up to the news of the collapse of Lehmann Brothers, the fourth largest investment bank in the US and Merrill Lynch, another iconic investment bank, was acquired by Bank of America. "In a period of less than eighteen months Wall Street had gone from celebrating its most profitable age to finding itself on the bank of an epochal devastation. Trillions of dollars in wealth had vanished, and the financial landscape was entirely reconfigured" (Sorkin 2010).[1]

Stock prices across the globe were on a downhill path throughout the year 2008. But something was terribly wrong this time. The ongoing recession soon turned into a doomsday situation as the whole world plunged into a full blown financial crisis. What followed were unanticipated and unprecedented memories of the Great Depression. Between October 2008 and March 2009, Dow Jones fell by 52.5%, a breath short of the record 54.5% between 1929 and 1931, at the height of the Great Depression. Dow Jones was not alone in this race to the bottom. In 2008, Britain's FTSE recorded its worst fall, a 31.3%; Shanghai's stock market recorded a 65.2% fall, Germany's DAX fell by 40.4%, SENSEX went down by 51.9% and Hong Kong stock market saw a fall of 48.3%.[2] For all who believed that the good times will never end, were in for a very, very rude shock. As the stock market plunged worldwide, the worst nightmare of investors started coming true. As the markets fell, then stopped as if catching a breath to its long way down and then fell again, the age old beliefs and rationales about the market that the market knows best started crumbling down all over. Best put in the words of Alan Greenspan, "the whole intellectual edifice, however, collapsed…".[3] As investors and traders saw the markets come crashing worldwide, economists and researchers,

---

[1] Sorkin A (2010) To big to fail. Penguin, India.

[2] Record stock market falls in 2008 http://bbc.co.uk/news/world/asia_pacific/. Accessed 24 August 2011.

[3] As quoted by Alan Greenspan before the committee of Government Oversight and Reform, October 23 2008. http://clipsandcomments.com/wp-content/uploads/2008/10/greenspan-testimony-20081023.pdf. Accessed 24 August 2011.

dumbfounded by the unexpected development, groped for a suitable explanation. And all answers led to one direction … a prolonged misinterpretation of the market behavior, which stood firmly on the traditional belief of the market's rationality. The stock market collapse had a severe ramification on not only other financial markets but also on people's lives. As by-products of the crisis, millions were soon jobless, homeless and suddenly poor all over the world. Everybody started believing that the "invisible hand" was dead.

Under these circumstances, it becomes important both on part of a researcher and a policy maker to understand what actually causes the turbulence. This book addresses the dynamics of stock prices and investigates into its underlying characteristics with focus on the last two stock market cycles. This study aims to investigate the nature of global stock market dynamics and their association during the financial crises between 1998 and 2011. It identifies two stock market cycles, the first between 1998 and 2003 and the second between 2006 and 2011. The second cycle has been more global in nature. Also, several structural breaks are identified during each cycle, for each market. The breaks in 2007 and especially in 2008 have been largely global in nature, hinting toward a dynamic interlinkage among the markets. The study delves deeper and finds evidence of latent structures in the global stock market around the stock market cycles. Some degree of internal association among the markets is also found to be present. Finally, the study investigates any possible chaotic nature of the stock markets. Results reveal a majority of the markets to be chaotic and all of them being deterministic in nature. This is likely to establish, particularly during the years of the global financial crisis, the inefficacy of the traditional asset pricing models as well as traditional policy tools which largely assume linearity.

Finally, the authors would like to thank Springer Briefs for publishing the manuscript and the anonymous referees for their valuable comments. However, it is us who should be held responsible for any flaw in the study.

Kolkata, India Gagari Chakrabarti
Gurgaon, India Chitrakalpa Sen

Contents

Chapter 1
Introduction

The charm of history and its enigmatic lesson consist in the fact that, from age to age, nothing changes and yet everything is completely different.

Aldous Huxley

Looking back into history, financial crises have always been the norm, rather than exceptions. Starting from the Tulip Mania in 1630, economic and financial vulnerabilities have generated waves of financial crises in the world economy. Not all the crises, by nature, however have been the same; rather they came in different forms and had different origins. While some of these remained confined to the domestic or regional boundaries, most of them reverberated, in no time, from the peripheries to the center with an ultimate devastating impact on the real economy. In this newfangled knowledge-driven financially integrated era such speedy spread of crisis is almost inevitable. The financial crises of early days, for example, those in France and Britain during the latter half of the 1710s remained confined to the regional territory. The first significant global crisis has probably been the panic of 1825 that initiated in Britain and eventually spread to the markets of Europe and Latin America. Since then, the global economy collapsed many a times. Panic spread from the US to countries of Europe, Asia and Africa in 1857. Apart from some regional crises in 1819, 1837, 1866 and 1893, global economy witnessed catastrophic crashes in 1873, 1907 and most importantly, in 1929. The debt crises during the 1980s and the Internet bubble during the last few years of the twentieth century were followed by a global financial meltdown that was on track since mid 2007. This crisis has often been described as the worst financial crisis since the one related to the Great Depression of the 1930s.

Financial crises are often seen as "Black swan": events that are fatal but improbable and extremely difficult, if not impossible, to predict (Taleb 2007). There is then, no single path that financial crises could follow. However, treating financial crises as "Black swan" ignores the fact that although the crisis gearing mechanism differs from one crash to another, they have much in common. Almost all crises are crises of confidence that begin when an initial boom turns into a bubble. But, what makes a boom take on the path of a bubble? A silver line does have its clouds and

(Huxley A (1952) The devils of Loudun. Chatto and Windus, London. 259)

G. Chakrabarti and C. Sen, *Anatomy of Global Stock Market Crashes*, SpringerBriefs in Economics, DOI: 10.1007/978-81-322-0463-3_1,

each boom brings into its train a potential bubble. A typical bubble begins with a 'precipitating factor' such as development of a new product, process or a theory that seems unique to the investors. This is usually followed by an 'amplification mechanism' generally in the form of assertions from media and like institutions that reinforce the view and the resulting stock price hike that convinces the investors about the emerging opportunities (Farlow 2002). People coming from almost every segment of society—from the business magnets to small investors; from the researchers and economists to the nonchalant observer of the economy seem to keep faith on the four most dangerous words in finance—"this time is different". Investors start believing that the traditional rules no longer apply, the current price rise is different from bubble, the market is flawless, and most importantly, the boom will continue even in the presence of irrational exuberance. The initial increase generates expectations of further increase and attracts new buyers—normally speculators. The rule of the game now becomes 'momentum'—stay close to the herd and track everyone else. Rational investors who realize that "not all of it is legal and not all of it is wealth" (Varian 2003) are crowded out or find it difficult to bet against the bubble to stop it in its track. The bubble bursts when the initial euphoria turns into retreat and triggering of a wreck usually have "no triggering news event…much of the drama of the market lies in its short term gyration" (Siegel 2000). The bubble bursts because stocks are going down as investors start selling them and people are selling them because stocks are going down; thereby initiating the crisis. The irrational exuberance in no time turns into irrational depression, "scarcely any one knows whom to trust" (Bagehot 1873). Regardless of how the upward journey is initiated or how people rush to join the speculative mania, the story repeats itself in all the financial crises. Thus, Roubini and Mihm (2010) prefer to call financial crises a "white swan": the fact that a crisis is looming large might well be predicted but the daunting task is to stop it in its track.

The ultimate devastating impact of any financial crises on the real economy has instigated researchers to explore the dynamics of the global stock markets, particularly, the possible dynamic inter-linkages (or, channels of contagion) among them. Moreover, the time is ripe to check whether global financial markets are inherently unstable which is why crashes are rules rather than aberrations. This study is a work that seeks to concentrate on this particular issue.

This study considers a period when the global economy has already been transformed into the so-called "new economy". The study has analyzed the significant crises that broke out in this knowledge-driven, knowledge-based and highly integrated global economy. Over a period of thirteen years, from 1998 to 2011, the study isolates two major crises that ultimately assumed global dimension having terrifying spill-over into the real economy. The first one (during 1999–2000) relates to the Internet bubble and the second one (during 2007–2008) has often been referred to as the worst financial crisis ever, since the one related to the great depression of 1929. The study is based on thirty stock markets from all over the globe. The market capitalization weighted bench market indexes that are representative of their own economy have been selected from each of these markets. From the *North American Region*, the study selects Dow Jones 30, S&P

500 and NASDAQ (US), Mexico IPC (Mexico) and S&P/TSX (Canada). From the *European* Region, the study selects CAC-40 (France), DAX (Germany), FTSE 100 (London), ATX (Austria), Madrid General (Spain), AEX General (Netherlands), Swiss Market (Switzerland), Bel20 (Belgium), OSE All Share (Norway), and Stockholm General (Stockholm). All Ordinaries Index (AORD) and NZSE 50 are chosen from *Australia* and *New Zealand*, respectively. MerVal (Argentina) and Bovespa (Brazil) are selected from the *South American* Region. From the *Asian* Region, the study picks BSE SENSEX (India); Shanghai Composite (China), Nikkei 225 (Japan), Hang Seng (Hong Kong), Straight Times (Singapore), Jakarta composite (Jakarta), KLSE composite (Malaysia), TWII (Taiwan) and Seoul Composite (Korea). CMA (Cairo) and TA100.TA (Tel Aviv) are considered from the *Middle East* and *African* countries.

While analyzing the nature of financial crisis in this "new economy" the study deals with some specific issues. Particularly, it seeks to answer the following set of questions:

- What has been the nature of stock price movements around the different stock market cycles?
- Is it possible to differentiate between any crisis that remains confined to the region and those which take up a global dimension?
- Is it possible to trace out presence of intra-regional and inter-regional association and/or global financial integration? And, if so, what is the source and nature of such contagion?
- Is it really the case that all financial crises by nature, have much in common among them?
- Are global markets intrinsically unstable where unpredictability, disorder and discontinuities are inherent and not aberrations? And, if that is so, what are its implications for investors and policy makers?

There have been some studies that have explored some of these issues albeit in an isolated manner. An empirical analysis at the global level addressing all such issues, particularly in the context of recent financial meltdowns, is however lacking in the field. In an earlier attempt, Chakrabarti (2010a, b) tried to analyze the dynamics of global market in terms of the crisis of 2007–2008 only. The focus of the study was essentially volatility transmission mechanism around the recent crisis period. The present study is a comprehensive, analytical study (instead of being theoretical only) into different stock market cycles, a comparison of their characteristics, the nature of inter-regional and intra-regional associations around the different cycles and the possible source of crises into the intrinsic nature of the global stock market dynamics, thus trying to fill the void in literature.

After this introductory chapter, the trajectory of the study will be as follows:

Chapter 2 is an analysis of global stock market behavior around the stock market cycles. Starting from a simple analysis of price movements it explores the global trends around these cycles and traces out the possible presence of intra-regional and inter-regional association and/or global financial integration. The possible intrinsic inter-relationship among global stock markets is then analyzed in a more technical way where the chapter explores whether and how the markets have passed through different volatility regimes across the cycles. To make it more interesting, the chapter inquires further whether volatility break dates coincide or at least follow some lead-lag relationship across markets.

Chapter 3 explores the latent structure in the global stock market by classifying constituent markets in different categories. Such market segmentation and comparison of the nature of latent structure around the cycles are useful in analysis of the nature and the extent of financial integration. After identifying the latent structure, the rest of the chapter seeks to address the following issues:

- Does any regional shock lead to or transmit into global shock? If so, what are the channels through which shocks reverberate from periphery to the center?
- In case of a purely regional shock, how do the stock markets within the region behave?
- In case of a global shock, what is the nature of inter-regional and intra-regional stock market dynamics?
- Finally, what is the source of volatility in these markets? Can the variability in a particular market be attributed to the variability of the other markets to which it is associated? Or, is it really the case of volatility being largely endogenous and a manifestation of the inherent instability or at best, of the knife-edge stability of any market? Chapter 4 deals with this issue in detail.

Chapter 4 explores whether the global markets are intrinsically unstable where unpredictability, disorder and discontinuities are inherent and not aberrations. This chapter follows the line of a growing body of literature and inquires the possible non-linear, particularly chaotic nature of the global stock markets. A chaotic system lacks any determinate equilibrium and is characterized by non-periodic limit cycles where fluctuations might be self-generating and endogenous to the system. Hence, in a chaotic stock market no external shock will be required to gear financial crisis at regular intervals which, in an integrated financial world, will reverberate across the globe in no time.

The study concludes by pointing toward the implications of the findings at investment and policy level.

References

Bagehot W (1873) Lombard Street: a description of the money market, 1920 edn. E.P Dutton, New York

Chakrabarti G (2010a) Dynamics of global stock market: crisis and beyond. Vdm-Verlag, Germany

Chakrabarti G (2010b) Propagator of global stock market volatility in recent years: Asian versus non-Asian markets. The Empirical Economics Letters 9(4):397–403

Farlow A (2002) The UK house price bubble. http:\\www.bubbles.com. Accessed 27 Nov 2003

Roubini N, Mihm S (2010) Crisis economics. Allen Lane Penguin Books, London

Siegel JJ (2000) What triggered the tech wreck? none of the usual suspects. http:\\www.bubble.com. Accessed 5 May 2004

Taleb NN (2007) The black swan: the impact of the highly improbable. Random House, New York

Varian HR (2003) Economics of information technology. University of California, Berkeley. http://citeseerx.ist.psu.edu/viewdoc/download?doi=10.1.1.8.3508&rep=rep1&type=pdf. Accessed 23 Mar 2005

Chapter 2
Stock Market Cycles and Volatility Regime Switch

The highest degree of prosperity … suddenly … plunged into embarrassment and distress.

Martin Van Buren

Abstract This chapter initiates the empirical dissection of stock market crises by an analysis of price movements and isolates two prominent stock market cycles over the study period. While the first cycle occurred during 1998–2005, a discernible second cycle took place from 2006 to 2011. The chapter analyzes the global trends around these cycles and explores the possible presence of intra-regional and inter-regional association and/or global financial integration. The intrinsic nature of different crises is further analyzed and compared in terms of volatility regime switch models where we inquire whether financial crises inevitably take the form of a structural break and whether such breaks follow some discernible pattern across the markets. The second cycle, rather than the first one appears to be truly 'global' and is marked by strong financial integration at the global level. Regional associations are however, not so robust. The association between financial crises and volatility breaks has been ambiguous and has varied from cycle to cycle. Such associations have been stronger over the second cycle where financial market changes have almost taken the form of volatility regime switch.

Keywords Financial crises · Stock market cycle · Structural break · Volatility regime · ICSS test · Dynamic interlinkage

2.1 Introduction

The boom-slump cycle of the stock market has been as old as capitalism itself. The fact that, boom-bust cycles had remained and will remain, however, hardly permits one to take these for granted. In reality we cannot afford to ignore such

Martin van Buren, address to Special Session of Congress, 4 September 1837. http://presidency.ucsb.edu/ws/index.php?pid=67234. Accessed 13 February 2007.

G. Chakrabarti and C. Sen, *Anatomy of Global Stock Market Crashes*, SpringerBriefs in Economics, DOI: 10.1007/978-81-322-0463-3_2,

cycles due to their potential threat to the financial markets as well as to the broader economy. A boom turns into a bust as "irrational exuberance" loses fuel and triggers massive panic leading sometimes to global financial meltdown. A growing body of literature emphasizes that the origin of such cycles might differ but the path followed by the global market during each of these cycles has remained the same. Every time, sheer lack of confidence and panic have overshadowed the initial euphoria and made the market struggle and plunge. Within this broad trend, however, it might be of relevance to trace the regional trends. Particularly, an exploration of whether and how the dynamics of and interlinkages within the global market change as it approaches a peak, slides from it and recovers could be of interest. A related and equally important issue could be an exploration of whether all the markets, irrespective of their levels of financial development, move similarly over different phases of stock market cycles. This is specifically what this chapter probes into.

The empirical anatomy of global market dynamics starts from a simple introspection of stock market movements. The study initiates by exploring the stock price movements across the different stock market cycles and seeks to trace possible presence of intra/inter regional association and/or global financial integration. Apart from such simple analysis of stock price movements, the study will explore the presence of volatility regime switch in stock markets across the globe. Specifically it will identify different volatility breaks in individual stock markets and will attempt to explore whether such volatility break dates are common across markets. This is particularly important because, any financial crisis is often considered as a switch in 'regime' that often manifests itself in a structural break in the market volatility. It would thus be interesting to explore whether the financial crises are necessarily associated with a volatility break or whether regime switches necessarily lead to financial crises. Moreover, this will help us analyze and compare the intrinsic nature of the different stock market crises. The possible inter-relationship among the global markets could be effectively analyzed by examining whether volatility break dates coincide or at least follow some lead-lag relationship across markets.

2.2 Two Significant Stock Market Cycles

Simple introspection of stock prices reveals the presence of three significant peaks and two significant troughs in the global market over the period from 1998 to 2011. In this study, the peaks are dates on which the market reaches a local maximum and troughs are those on which any market hits its local minimum in terms of price. On the basis of price movements, the study isolates two significant stock market cycles in the global stock market. While the first cycle occurred from 1998 to 2003, the second cycle covered the period of 2006 to 2011.

2.2.1 The First Cycle Revisited

Analysts might find it difficult to label the first cycle as 'truly' global because of its failure to have an all-embracing impact on the global stock market. Out of the thirty markets selected, the cycle remained significant in only twenty of them. The crisis failed to hit the African (Cairo) and the Middle East (Tel Aviv) markets, and the Asia–Pacific markets such as Australia, New Zealand and Indonesia could avoid the heat of this cycle. A few markets from the European region (such as Austria, Oslo and Stockholm) and the American region (such as Mexico and Argentina) too managed to escape the crisis. The impact of the cycle, however, has been tremendous on the markets on which it hit hard. In six out of these twenty markets, affected intensely by the crisis, the peak-price attained during the cycle has remained the all-time high. For these six markets of Taiwan, Japan, UK, France, Austria and the US (NASDAQ only) the first cycle brought about incredible prosperity that could not be outshined even in the next 13 years. Moreover, the slump associated with the cycle has been the all-time dip for fifteen out of these twenty markets. It has been the worst crisis that these economies have seen. The journey towards the first peak was initiated by the European markets. The Swiss market was the first to reach the peak in July 1998 followed by Belgium that reached the summit in January 1999. Specifically, it is since December 1999 that markets starting from the London stock market began to reach their respective peaks one after another. However, it is difficult to trace out any regional pattern in this movement. The process of reaching peaks continued for a sufficiently long period of time. It took almost four and a half years (from July 1998 to April 2002) for all the markets to reach their respective peaks. The process of reaching the trough had been more of a global phenomenon rather than a regional one. The markets started hitting their slumps since April 2002. Within a short span of one year all the twenty markets reached their respective trough. Out of these twenty markets, three hit their slumps in September–October 2001. In October 2002, six markets touched their minima with five (including the three US indexes) of them reaching slump simultaneously on 9 October 2002. The nose-diving completed in March–April 2003, when eight markets hit their slumps. Of these eight markets, five from the European region touched their lowest on 12 March 2003. Thus, the first recession considered in this study has been a truly global phenomenon. However, some regional association might be expected to be present within the European region and among the US markets. The peaks and troughs associated with the first cycle in global market are shown in Fig. 2.1.

2.2.2 The Second Cycle Revisited

The second cycle has remained prominent in all the thirty markets selected. For seventeen markets, out of the chosen thirty, prices have been all-time high

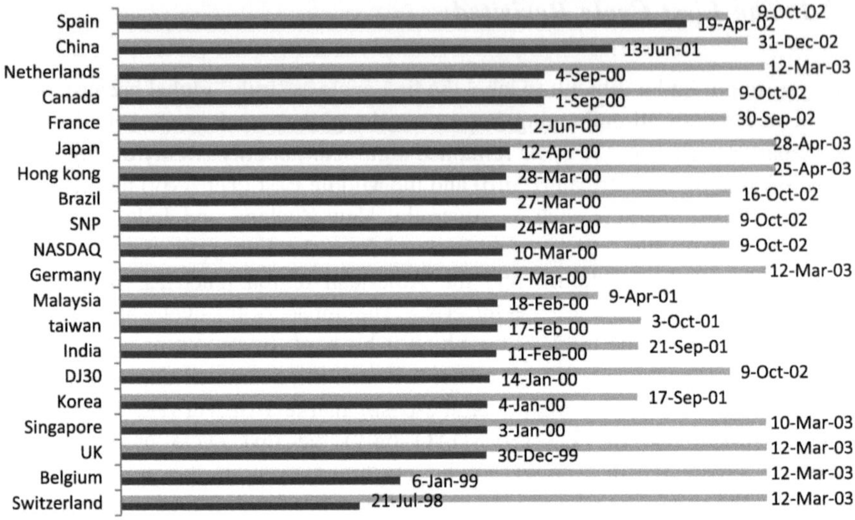

Fig. 2.1 First peak and first trough in global stock market

around this peak. For thirteen markets, prices have been all-time low around the slump. Clearly, the prosperity that it brought about was enormous while the distress that followed was toe-curling. As is evident from the dates of reaching the respective peaks, the European markets (and two Asia Pacific markets) were once again to initiate the move. The nature of the movement around the second cycle has been quite different from the first one in the sense that stock market movements toward peak were much more 'global' in nature. In contrast to the first cycle, the process of reaching their respective peaks by the stock markets in the second phase completed within a relatively shorter period of time. The process continued for a period of one year starting from May 2007. The markets reached their respective peaks either simultaneously or within a short span of time. Eleven markets reached their respective peaks within a short span of two months starting from May 2007. New Zealand and Belgium reached their respective peaks on two consecutive days. Switzerland and France reached their peaks on the same day (that is on 1 June 2007). Same was the case for the Japan-Austria market pair. They reached their peaks on 9 July 2007. Stock markets of Stockholm and Germany reached summit on 16 July 2007. Nine markets reached their peaks in October 2007. Once again, Dow Jones and S&P reached their peaks simultaneously on 9 October. Tel Aviv and Taiwan reached their peak on 29 October. NASDAQ, Argentinean and Korean markets reached their respective peaks on 31 October. Asian markets attained their individual peaks in two phases: the first one was in October 2007 and the other one was in January 2008. The process of hitting the slump has been really a global phenomenon. Out of the thirty markets, twenty-one reached their respective slumps in March 2009. More interestingly, nine out of these markets touched

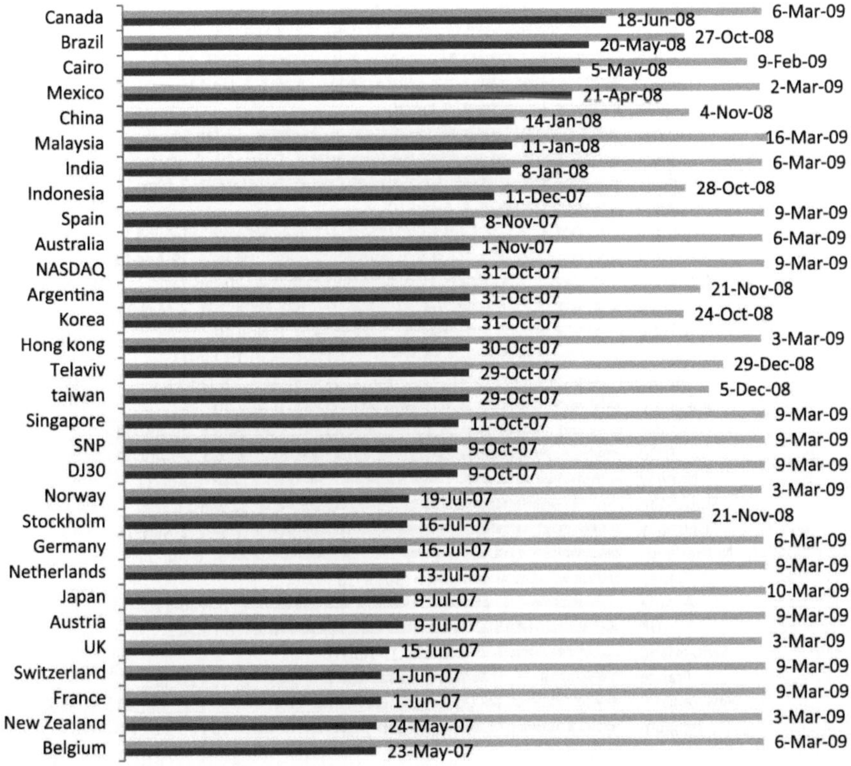

Fig. 2.2 Second peak and second trough in global stock market

their trough on 9 March; five hit slump on 6 March and three dipped on 3 March 2009. Thus, like the first cycle considered earlier, while some regional association could be expected to exist during the pre-crisis period of this second phase, the recession has been more of a global nature. Figure 2.2 depicts the second peak and second trough in the global stock market.

2.2.3 The Peak in the Recent Years

The markets have started recovering since March 2009. They have approached their respective peaks once again in more recent years. This is depicted in Fig. 2.3. For seven markets, prices have been all-time high around this peak. However, due to lack of sufficient data in recent years, it would be too early to explain it as the initiation of the third cycle. Our study clubs the period from 2009 to 2011 in the second phase of stock market movement. Simple introspection of stock price movement hints toward possible presence of some intra-regional association,

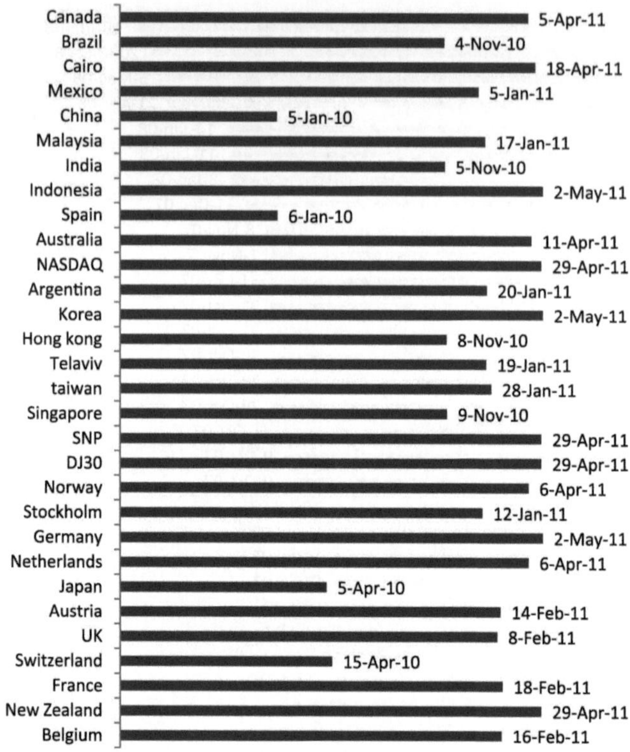

Fig. 2.3 Third peak in global stock market

particularly within the Asian region, European region and the US region. Some kind of lead-lag relationship might also be expected to hold.

2.2.4 *Three Peaks and Two Troughs*

A comparison among the stock prices that the markets attained during their respective peaks and slumps might be of interest in this context (Fig. 2.4). The nineteen markets that have passed through both the cycles can be clubbed under three categories. For eleven of them, the second peak has been more significant than the first one in the sense that prices have been significantly higher around the second peak. The difference has been maximum for the Indian market. Out of these eleven markets as many as six come from the Asian region. For some European markets and the S&P index, prices around the two peaks have been more or less the same. For the remaining markets, the first peak has been more significant.

A comparison of the two slumps (Fig. 2.5) reveals that prices around the first trough has been much lower compared to the second one in most of the markets. On average, prices have been 47% higher around the second trough. The difference

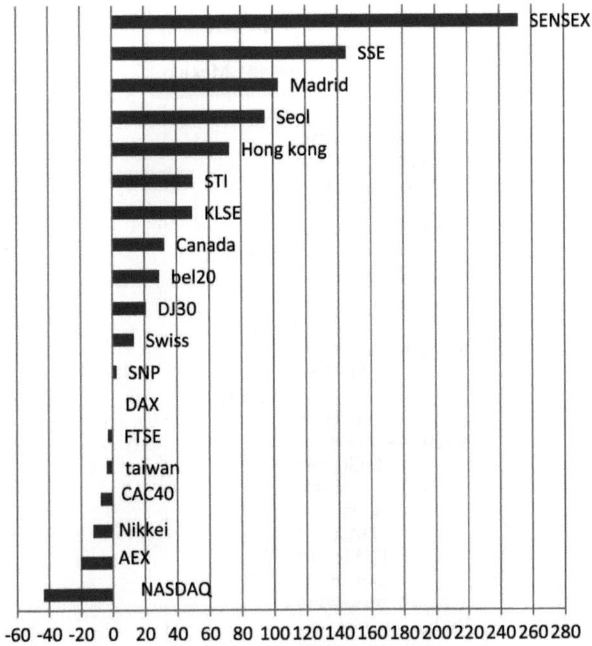

Fig. 2.4 Price difference between the first and second peaks (in percentage)

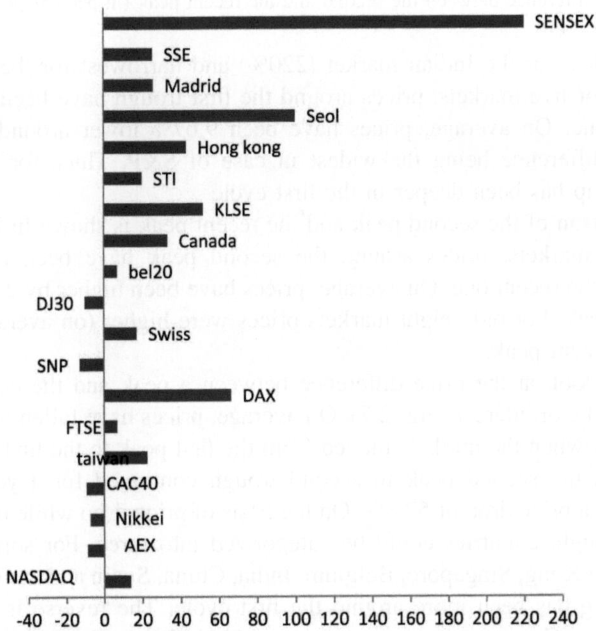

Fig. 2.5 Price difference between the first and second trough (in percentage)

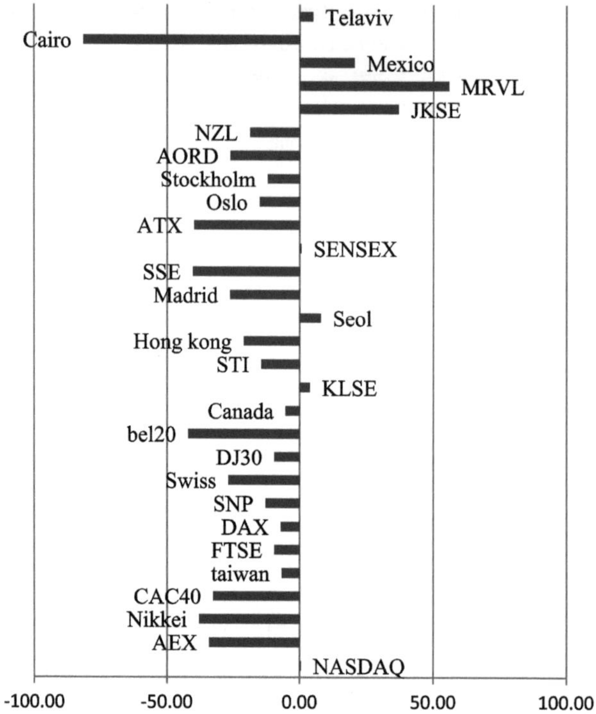

Fig. 2.6 Price difference between the second and the recent peak (in percentage)

has been widest for the Indian market (220%) and narrowest for the UK market (6%). Only for five markets, prices around the first trough have been higher than the second one. On average, prices have been 9.67% lower around the second trough, the difference being the widest in case of S&P. Thus, for most of the markets, slump has been deeper in the first cycle.

A comparison of the second peak and the recent peak is shown in Fig. 2.6. For most of the markets, prices around the second peak have been much higher compared to the recent one. On average, prices have been higher by 24.8% around the second peak. For only eight markets prices were higher (on average by 16%) around the recent peak.

Finally, a look at the price difference between a peak and the corresponding trough might be of interest (Fig. 2.7). On average, prices have fallen by 55.34% in almost 1 year when the markets moved from the first peak to the first trough. The journey from the second peak to second trough continued for 1 year and was associated by a price drop of 57.8%. On the basis of price drop while moving from a peak to trough, countries could be categorized into three. For some countries (such as Hong Kong, Singapore, Belgium, India, China, Spain and the US markets) price shedding has been more around the first cycle. The reverse is true for the markets such as Germany, Taiwan, Austria and NASDAQ. For few other markets price change has been more or less the same around the two cycles.

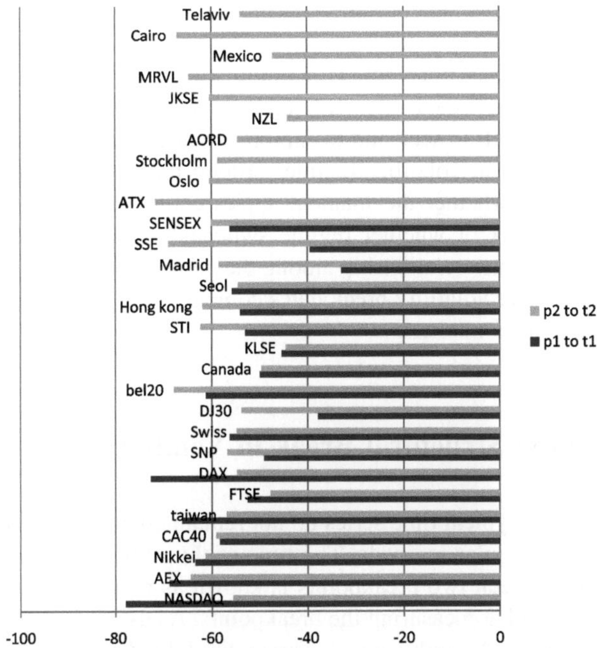

Fig. 2.7 Price shedding during the journey from peak to trough (in percentage)

Thus, simple introspection of stock price movements reveals some trends that need further analysis. To summarize:

- Two prominent stock market cycles could be traced in the global market over a period of 13 years from 1998 to 2011.
- The second cycle (covering the period from 2006 to 2011), rather than the first one (1998–2004) has been more general, or 'global' in nature.
- For most of the markets, the prices around the second peak (around 2007–2008) have been the all-time high.
- For most of the markets, the prices around the first trough (around 2002–2003) have been the all-time low.
- It could hardly be expected to have any regional pattern in stock price movements during the first cycle. However, some regional association might be expected during the second cycle, particularly when the markets were approaching their respective peaks. Recessions have been truly global in both the cycles, although the extent of 'being global' varies.
- Since during both the cycles, markets reached their respective peaks (and troughs) either simultaneously or in consecutive days, some kind of financial integration (or, lead-lag relationship) might be expected to prevail in the global market.

With these findings in the back of our mind, we now proceed to explore the possible intrinsic inter-relationship among stock markets of the world in a more technical way. To supplement our previous analysis, we now look for the presence or otherwise of volatility breaks in these markets within the study period. This is particularly because, any financial crisis could well be thought of as a switch in regime that is often reflected in a structural break in the market volatility. The study now extends itself to seek and to explore whether and how the markets have passed through different volatility regimes around these stock market cycles. In that way, we check whether the financial crises could necessarily be associated with a volatility break or whether regime switches necessarily lead to financial crises. The possible inter-relationship among the global markets has been analyzed by examining whether volatility break dates coincide or at least follow some lead-lag relationship across markets.

2.3 Detection of Structural Break in Volatility

The parameters of a typical time series do not remain constant over time. It makes paradigm shifts in regular intervals. The time of this shift is the structural break. And the period between two breakpoints is known as a regime. There have been several studies aimed at measuring the breakpoints. As usual, majority of them are in the stock market. As only the algorithm used to detect the breakpoints is important rather than the underlying time series, the following section discusses the studies with important breakthroughs in the algorithm irrespective of the market.

The first group of studies was able to detect only one unknown structural breakpoint. Perron (1990), Hansen (1990, 1992), Banerjee et al. (1992), Perron and Vogelsang (1992), Chu and White (1992), Andrews (1993), Andrews and Ploberger (1994), Perron (1997a) did some major works in this area. Studies by Nelson and Plosser (1982), Perron (1989), Zivot and Andrews (1992) tested unit root in presence of structural break. Bai (1994, 1997) considered the distributional properties of the break dates.

The second group of studies was an improvement over the first as it was able to detect multiple structural breaks in a financial time series, most importantly endogenous break points. Significant contributions were made by Zivot and Andrews (1992). Perron (1989, 1997b), Bai and Perron (2003), Lumsdaine and Papell (1997) tests for unit root allowing for two breaks in the trend function. Hansen (2001) considers multiple breaks, although he considers the breaks to be exogenously given.

The major breakthrough was the study by Inclan and Tiao (1994), who proposed a test to detect shifts in unconditional variance that is the volatility. This test is used extensively in financial time series to identify breaks in volatility (Wilson et al. 1996; Aggarwal et al. 1999; Huang and Yang 2001). This test was later modified by Sansó et al. (2004) to account for conditional variance as well.

Hsu et al. (1974) proposed in their study a model with nonstationary variance which is subjected to changes. This is probably the first work involving structural breaks in variance. Hsu's later works in (1977, 1979 and in 1982) were aimed at detecting a single break in variance in a time series. Abraham and Wei (1984) discussed methods of identifying a single structural shift in variance. An improvement came in the study of Baufays and Rasson (1985) who addressed the issue with multiple breakpoints in their paper. Tsay (1988) also discussed ARMA models allowing for outliers and variance changes and proposed a method for detecting the breakpoint in variance. More recently, Cheng (2009) provided an algorithm to detect multiple structural breakpoints for a change in mean as well as a change in variance.

This study does not explicitly incorporate any regime switching model but considers the period between two breaks as a regime. Schaller and Norden (1997) used Markov Switching model to find very strong evidence of regime switch in CRSP value-weighted monthly stock market returns from 1929 to 1989. Marcucci (2005) used a regime switching GARCH model to forecast volatility in S&P 500 which is characterized by several regime switches. Structural breaks and regime switch is addressed by Ismail and Isa (2006) who used a SETAR type model to test structural breaks in Malaysian Ringgit, Singapore Dollar and Thai Baht.

Theoretically, volatility break dates are basically structural breaks in variance of a given time series. Structural breaks are often defined as persistent and pronounced macroeconomic shifts in the data generating process. Usually, the probability of observing any structural break increases as we expand the period of study. The methodology used in this chapter is the line of analysis that was followed by Inclan and Tiao (1994). In the following section, we are briefly recapitulating the methodology.

We may start from a simple AR (1) process as that described in (2.1) and (2.2).

$$y_t = \alpha + \rho y_{t-1} + \varepsilon_t \tag{2.1}$$

$$E\varepsilon_t^2 = \sigma^2 \tag{2.2}$$

Here ε_t is a time series of serially uncorrelated shocks. If the series is stationary, the parameters α, ρ and σ^2 are constant over time. By definition, a structural break occurs if at least one of the parameters changes permanently at some point in time (Hansen 2001). The time point where the parameter changes value is often termed as a "break date". According to Brooks (2002), structural breaks are irreversible in nature. The reasons behind occurrence of structural breaks, however, are not very specified. Economic and non-economic (or even unidentifiable) reasons are equally likely to bring about structural break in volatility (Valentinyi- Endrész 2004).

2.3.1 Detection of Multiple Structural Breaks in Variance: The ICSS Test

The Iterative Cumulative Sum of Squares (or the ICSS) algorithm by Inclan and Tiao (1994) can very well detect sudden changes in unconditional variance for a stochastic process. Hence, the test is often used to detect multiple shifts in volatility. The algorithm starts from the premise that over an initial period, the time series under consideration displays a stationary variance. The variance changes following a shock to the system and continues to be stationary till it experiences another shock in the future. This process is repeated over time till we could identify all the breaks. Structural breaks can effectively capture regime switches (Altissimo and Corradi 2003; Gonzalo and Pitarakis 2002; Valentinyi-Endrész 2004). The different tests for identifying volatility breaks isolate dates where conditional volatility moves from one stationary level to another. The idea is similar to those lying behind the Markov regime switching models, where a system jumps from one volatility regime to another.

2.3.1.1 The Original Model: Breaks in Unconditional Variance

The original model of Inclan and Tiao (1994) is reproduced as follows:

Let $C_k = \sum_{t=1}^{k} a_t^2, k = 1, \ldots, T$ is the cumulative sum of squares for a series of independent observations $\{a_t\}$, where $a_t \sim iidN(0, \sigma^2)$ and $t = 1, 2, \ldots, T$, σ^2 is the unconditional variance.

$$\sigma^2 = \begin{cases} \tau_0, 1 < t < \kappa_1 \\ \tau_1, \kappa_1 < t < \kappa_2 \\ \ldots \\ \tau_{N_T}, \kappa_{N_T} < t < T \end{cases} \tag{2.3}$$

where $1 < \kappa_1 < \kappa_2 < \cdots < \kappa_{N_T} < T$ are the break points that is where the breaks in variances occur. N_T is the total number of such changes for T observations. Within each interval, the variance is $\tau_j^2, j = 0, 1, \ldots, N_T$.

The centralized or normalized cumulative sum of squares is denoted by D_k where

$$D_k = \frac{C_k}{C_T} - \frac{k}{T} D_0 = D_T = 0 \tag{2.4}$$

C_T is the sum of squared residuals for the whole sample period. If there is no volatility shift D_k will oscillate around zero. With a change in variance, it will drift upward or downward and will exhibit a pattern going out of some specified boundaries (provided by a critical value based on the distribution of D_k) with high probability. If at some k, say k^*, the maximum absolute value of D_k, given by $\max_k \left| \sqrt{T/2D_k} \right|$ exceeds the critical value, the null hypothesis of constant variance is rejected and k^* will be regarded as an estimate of the change point. Under variance homogeneity, $\sqrt{T/2D_k}$ behaves like a Brownian bridge asymptotically.

For multiple breakpoints, however, the usefulness of the D_k function is questionable due to the "masking effect". To avoid this, Inclan and Tiao designed an iterative algorithm that uses successive application of the D_k function at different points in the time series to look for possible shift in volatility.

2.3.1.2 Modified ICSS Test: Breaks in Conditional Variance

The modified ICSS test will now be reproduced and used in this study. Sansó et al. (2004) found significant size distortions for the ICSS test in presence of excessive kurtosis and conditional heteroscedasticity. This makes original ICSS test invalid in context of financial time series that are often characterized by fat tails and conditional heteroscedasticity. As a remedial measure, they introduced two tests to explicitly consider the fourth moment properties of the disturbances and the conditional heteroscedasticity.

The first test, or the $\kappa_1$test, makes the asymptotic distribution free of nuisance parameters for *iid* zero mean random variables.

$$\kappa_1 = \sup_k \left| T^{-1/2} B_k \right|, \quad k = 1, \ldots, T \tag{2.5}$$

$$B_k = \frac{C_k - \frac{k}{T} C_T}{\sqrt{\hat{\eta}_4 - \hat{\sigma}^4}}, \; \hat{\eta}_4 = T^{-1} \sum\nolimits_{t=1}^{T} \varepsilon_t^4 \text{ and } \hat{\sigma}^4 = T^{-1} C_T$$

This statistic is free of any nuisance parameter. The second test, the $\kappa_2$test solves the problems of fat tails and persistent volatility.

$$\kappa_2 = \sup_k \left| T^{-1/2} G_k \right| \tag{2.6}$$

where $G_k = \hat{\omega}_4^{-\frac{1}{2}} (C_k - \frac{k}{T} C_T)$

$\hat{\omega}_4$ is a consistent estimator of ω_4. A nonparametric estimator of ω_4 can be expressed as:

$$\hat{\omega}_4 = \frac{1}{T} \sum\nolimits_{i=1}^{T} (\varepsilon_t^2 - \hat{\sigma}^2)^2 + \frac{2}{T} \sum\nolimits_{l=1}^{m} \omega(l, m) \sum\nolimits_{t=1}^{T} (\varepsilon_t^2 - \hat{\sigma}^2)(\varepsilon_{t-1}^2 - \hat{\sigma}^2) \tag{2.7}$$

$\omega(l, m)$ is a lag window, and is defined as $\omega(l, m) = [1 - l/(m + 1)]$. The bandwidth m is chosen by the Newey-West (1994) technique. The κ_2 test is more powerful than the original Inclan-Tiao test or even the κ_1 test and is best fit for our purpose.

2.3.2 Volatility Breaks in Global Stock Market

On the basis of the modified ICSS test, the study has identified different volatility break dates in the global stock market. The break dates are presented in the following tables. Break dates are shown for two subperiods. The first subperiod, defined around the first cycle, considers the period from 1998 to 2004 (Table 2.1). The second subperiod defined over the second cycle ranges from 2005 to 2011 (Table 2.2).

Table 2.1 Volatility break dates in phase 1

Germany	12-Jun-02	16-May-03	27-Oct-03			
Austria	23-Mar-00					
Belgium	10-Jun-02	20-May-03	3-Jun-04			
France	31-May-02	29-Oct-02	10-Mar-03	9-Apr-03	10-Oct-03	
UK	10-Jun-02	1-Nov-02	11-Jul-03			
Oslo	5-Dec-02					
Stockholm	7-Apr-03	20-Aug-04				
Spain	9-Jul-03					
Australia	28-Apr-03					
Taiwan	9-Mar-00	14-Feb-01	28-Aug-03	16-Mar-04	23-Aug-04	
Hong Kong	15-Oct-98	14-Nov-01	23-Jun-04			
Indonesia	28-Oct-99	2-Jun-04				
Malaysia	12-Aug-99					
Japan	16-Dec-03					
India	27-Apr-01					
Seoul	25-Apr-00	1-Nov-02				
Singapore	13-Feb-98	26-Aug-98	19-Feb-99	1-Mar-02	18-Nov-03	27-Apr-04
Brazil	26-May-99					
Canada	20-Apr-01	8-Jul-02	17-Dec-02			
Argentina	15-Jul-99	29-Jun-01	15-Jul-02	17-Jun-04		
Mexico	4-Jan-01	26-Nov-02				
Cairo	24-Nov-99	27-Nov-00	26-Sep-01			
Tel aviv	21-Jan-04					
DJ30	2-Jul-02	18-Oct-02	1-Apr-03	24-Jul-03		
NASDAQ	24-Aug-98	9-Mar-00	20-Apr-01	1-Apr-03	17-Aug-04	
S&P	13-Jun-02	16-Oct-02	1-Apr-03	30-Sep-03		

Volatility breaks during phase 1

The number of break dates has been the maximum in the Singapore stock market (six breaks altogether) followed by the markets of France, Taiwan and the NASDAQ (five breaks). The other two indexes of the US market (namely, S&P and Dow Jones) and the Argentinean market are characterized by four breaks. The markets of Germany, Belgium, UK, Hong Kong, Canada and Cairo have experienced three volatility breaks each. Stockholm, Indonesia, Seoul, Mexico and Tel Aviv experienced two volatility breaks in their stock markets. The remaining eight markets, namely, Austria, Oslo, Spain, Australia, Malaysia, Japan, India and Brazil experienced a single break in volatility over the study period. Thus, phase 1 has remained a period of excessive volatility change for only a few markets.

The first volatility break date occurred during 1998. This was, however, not a common break date. The stock markets of Singapore, Hong Kong and US (NASDAQ only) experienced breaks in volatility in 1998, but not simultaneously. The second break date for Singapore and the first break date for NASDAQ, however, are very close to each other.

Table 2.2 Volatility break dates in phase 2

Germany	11-Jan-08	2-Oct-08	5-Dec-08	14-Jul-09	23-Jul-10		
Austria	25-Apr-06	2-Sep-08	5-Dec-08	23-Jun-09	30-Jun-10		
Belgium	10-May-06						
France	16-Jul-07	17-Sep-08	5-Dec-08				
UK	16-Jul-07	11-Sep-08	5-Dec-08	20-May-09			
Oslo	3-Oct-05						
Stockholm	10-May-06	2-Sep-08	8-Dec-08	12-May-09			
Australia	18-Mar-05	2-May-06					
Taiwan	24-Jul-07	28-Aug-08	12-Dec-08	23-Jun-09	5-Jul-10		
HongKong	30-Mar-06						
Indonesia	25-Jul-07	4-Jun-10					
Japan	27-Dec-07	8-Apr-09					
New Zealand	13-Dec-07	16-Feb-10	30-Sep-10				
India	5-Oct-07	17-Jul-09					
China	6-Dec-06	18-Nov-09					
Singapore	4-May-06	24-Jul-07	2-Sep-08	18-May-09	21-Aug-09		
Canada	30-Sep-05	20-Jul-07	5-Sep-08	28-Nov-08	20-Mar-09	14-Aug-09	6-Nov-09
Argentina	2-Sep-08	28-Nov-08	14-Jul-09				
Mexico	30-Dec-05	11-Sep-08	28-Nov-08	20-May-09	31-May-10		
Tel aviv	9-Jun-05						
DJ30	6-Jul-07	11-Sep-08	1-Dec-08	29-May-09			
NASDAQ	20-Jul-07	11-Sep-08	5-Dec-08	29-May-09			
S&P	27-Jul-06						

The three Asian markets (namely, Indonesia, Malaysia and Singapore), two markets of Latin America (namely, Brazil and Argentina) and Cairo stock market experienced a volatility break during 1999. The breaks, however, are neither simultaneous nor following any specific pattern. The volatility break dates found during 1998 and 1999 are thus not common break dates in the global market.

The volatility breaks during the year of 2000 were significant only in the markets of Austria, Taiwan, Seoul, Cairo and NASDAQ. The markets of Taiwan and the US experienced, for the first time since 1998, a volatility break on the same date (namely 9 March 2000). The other dates, however, do not coincide.

The stock markets of Taiwan, Hong Kong, India, Argentina, Mexico, Cairo and the US (NASDAQ only) experienced breaks in volatility during 2001. The dates however, do not coincide.

The stock markets of France, UK, Seoul, Singapore, Argentina, and the US (namely, DJ30 and S&P) experienced breaks in volatility during 2002. Of these markets, the French, the London and the two US markets experienced two breaks each during the year. Moreover, the break dates in the London market lag those in the French market by exactly one month in each case. The two US markets and Argentina experienced volatility breaks in July 2002, where as the US markets shared a break with the French market in October 2002. While S&P and UK experienced break in June 2002, Seoul and London experienced break in November 2002. The volatility breaks during 2002 are thus, more simultaneous in nature.

Thirteen markets experienced breaks during 2003. Of them the two US indexes and the German market experienced two breaks during the year. The French market experienced as many as three breaks over the time. The French market was the first to experience a volatility break in March. It experienced another break in quick succession during April 2003 along with the three US markets (where the break dates coincide) and the markets of Stockholm, and Australia. Two European markets of Germany and Belgium experienced breaks in May. UK, Spain and Dow Jones experienced break in July. It was only in August that any Asian market (namely Taiwan) could experience its break for the first time in 2003. Singapore and Japan remained the other two Asian markets to have any breaks during 2003. Thus, it was mainly the European and the US markets that went through volatility regimes during 2003. For these markets some breaks have been simultaneous or have occurred in quick succession.

The stock markets of the US (NASDAQ), Argentina, Singapore, Indonesia, Hong Kong, Taiwan, Stockholm and Belgium experienced volatility breaks during 2004. The breaks occurred during March 2004 and August 2004 and have been simultaneous in nature.

Tel Aviv stock market has been the only one to experience a volatility break during 2005.

The period of 1998 to 2005 was thus characterized by the presence of many volatility breaks in the global stock market. It is however, very difficult to trace out any pattern in these breaks. The breaks, in most of the cases have not been simultaneous or common to all the markets. Moreover, while the breaks are not global, there is hardly any regional pattern.

Volatility breaks during phase 2

The second phase (2005–2011) has been characterized by many volatility regimes in the global stock market. Out of the thirty markets selected as many as twenty three experienced volatility switches during this phase. The number of break dates has been the maximum (seven) in the Canadian market. The markets of Germany, Austria, Taiwan, Singapore and Mexico experienced five volatility breaks each over the period. Each of the markets of the UK, Stockholm and the US (Dow Jones and NASDAQ, respectively) has been characterized by four breaks in volatility. The markets of France, New Zealand and Argentina have experienced three volatility breaks each. While the stock markets of Australia, Indonesia, Japan, India and China each experienced two breaks, markets of Belgium, Oslo, Hong Kong, Tel Aviv and the US (S&P) were characterized by single volatility break date.

The break dates during 2005 were not global in true sense. The year of 2005 was mostly a period of tranquility in the global stock market. Only the five markets of Tel Aviv, Oslo, Canada, Mexico and Australia experienced volatility break in 2005. More interestingly, the first two markets have experienced no more volatility breaks during the second phase of study.

The year of 2006 was characterized by volatility breaks in the stock markets of Austria, Belgium, Stockholm, Australia, Hong Kong, China, Singapore and the US (namely, S&P). Of these markets, four experienced a break date in May 2006.

The volatility breaks in 2007, particularly in July 2007 have been global in true sense. Nine markets experienced a volatility break in July 2007, of which some break dates coincide. Some sort of lead-lag relationship might exist among the other break dates in the world market.

The nature of break dates during 2008 has been particularly interesting. The stock markets of Austria, France, UK, Stockholm, Singapore, Canada, Mexico and the US (except for S&P) experienced volatility breaks in September 2008. Of these markets, Austria, Stockholm and Singapore each had a break on 2 September. The markets of UK, Singapore, Mexico and the US experienced break on 11 September. Another break date occurred during November–December, 2008. Canada, Argentina and Mexico attained their respective volatility breaks on 28 November 2008. Germany, Austria, France, UK, and NASDAQ reached their break dates on 5 December 2008. Stockholm, Taiwan the US market (namely, DJ30) also attained their respective break dates in December 2008. Thus, the break dates during 2008 are once again global. Some regional pattern and some lead-lag movements (if not simultaneous) could be easily traced in the global market.

Some lead-lag and even simultaneous movements are once again visible during 2009. Markets passed through different volatility regimes during a period from March 2009 to November 2009. Markets of the UK, Stockholm, Singapore, Mexico and the US (namely DJ30 and NASDAQ) experienced volatility breaks during May 2009. Many markets experienced breaks in July and August 2009.

The markets of Mexico, New Zealand, Indonesia, Taiwan, Austria and Germany experienced breaks during 2010. Some lead-lag movements might once again be expected in the global stock market over this period.

The two phases compared

The nature of volatility breaks during the study period reveals something interesting. Over the two cycles considered in the study, the global markets have experienced significant volatility changes. Any stock market cycle defined around a significant crisis and its aftermath has been characterized by significant and vigorous volatility changes in the global stock markets. Moreover, the markets worst-hit by such crises have gone through series of volatility regimes within a very short span of time. The association between financial crises and volatility breaks, however, has been ambiguous. While significant financial market changes (including, of course, crises) have often been associated with volatility breaks, the mere presence of volatility breaks has not ever been sufficient to identify a peak or a trough in global stock market. Moreover, the extent and degree of such association has varied over cycles. During the first phase the association between volatility regime switch and financial crises has been quite weak. The associations were stronger over the second phase of study where financial market changes have almost taken the form of volatility regime switch. The analysis has further hinted toward possible presence of some regional association and strong financial integration at the global level over the two cycles considered in the study, particularly during the second one that has been truly global in nature. It could now be of interest to analyze the nature of such associations in greater detail and to identify channels through which a regional crisis might spill over to the rest of the world and assume global dimension. Such an exploration, however, requires a study of latent structure in the global stock market and that is where we move next.

References

Abraham B, Wei W (1984) Inferences about the parameters of a time series model with changing variance.Metrika 31(1):183–194
Aggarwal R, Inclan C, Leal R (1999) Volatility in emerging stock markets. J Finan Quant Anal 34:33–55
Altissimo F, Corradi V (2003) Strong rules for detecting the number of breaks in a time series. J Econ 117(2): 207–244
Andrews DWK (1993) Tests for parameter instability and structural change with unknown change point. Econometrica 61:821–856
Andrews DWK, Ploberger W (1994) Optimal tests when a nuisance parameter is present only under the alternative. Econometrica 62:1383–1414
Bai J (1994) Least squares estimation of a shift in linear processes. J Time Ser Anal 15:453–472
Bai J (1997) Estimation of a change point in multiple regression models. Rev Econ Stat 79:551–563
Bai J, Perron P (2003) Computation and analysis of multiple structural change models. J Appl Econom 18(1):1–22
Banerjee A, Lumsdaine RL, Stock JH (1992) Recursive and sequential tests of the unit root and trend break hypotheses: theory and international evidence. J Bus Econ Stat 10:271–287
Baufays P, Rasson JP (1985) Variance changes in autoregressive models. In: Anderson OD (ed) Time series analysis: theory and practice, 7th edn. North Holland Publisher, New York
Brooks C (2002) Introductory econometrics for finance. Cambridge University Press, Cambridge
Cheng T (2009) An efficient algorithm for estimating a change-point. Stat Probab Lett 79:559–565
Chu CSJ, White H (1992) A direct test for changing trend. J Bus Econ Stat 10:189–199
Gonzalo J, Pitarakis JY (2002) Estimation and model selection based inference in single and multiple threshold models. J Econom 110:319–352
Hansen BE (1990) Lagrange multiplier tests for parameter instability in non-linear models. Unpublished manuscript, University of Rochester, Rochester, New York. http://www.ssc.wisc.edu/~bhansen/paper/LMTests.pdf. Accessed 21 Sep 2010
Hansen BE (1992) Test for instability with I(1) processes. J Bus Econ Stat 10:321–335
Hansen BE (2001) The new econometrics of structural change: dating breaks in U.S. labor productivity. J Econ Perspect 15(4):117–128
Hsu DA (1977) Testing for variance shifts at unknown time point. Appl Stat 26:279–284
Hsu DA (1979) Detecting shifts of parameter in gamma sequences with applications to stock price and air traffic flow analysis. J Am Stat Assoc 74(365):31–40
Hsu DA (1982) A Bayesian robust detection of shift in the risk structure of stock market returns. J Am Stat Assoc 77(377):29–39
Hsu A, Miller RB, Wichern DW (1974) On the stable Paretian behavior of stock-market prices. J Am Stat Assoc 69(345):108–113

Huang B, Yang C (2001) The impact of settlement time on the volatility of stock market revisited: an application of the iterated cumulative sums of squares detection method for changes of variance. Appl Econ Lett 8:665–668

Inclan C, Tiao GC (1994) Use of cumulative sums of squares for retrospective detection of changes of variance. J Am Stat Assoc 89:913–923

Ismail MT, Isa Z (2006) Modelling exchange rates using regime switching models. Sains Malaysiana 35(2):55–62

Lumsdaine RL, Papell DH (1997) Multiple trend breaks and the unit root hypothesis. Rev Econ Statist 79: 223–230

Marcucci J (2005) Forecasting stock market volatility with regime-switching GARCH models. Stud Nonlinear Dynam Econom 9(4), Article 6: 1–53

Nelson CR, Plosser CI (1982) Trends and random walks in macroeconomic time series. J Monet Econ 10:139–162

Newey KW, West KD (1994) Automatic lag selection in covariance matrix estimation. Rev Econ Stud 61(4):631–653

Perron P (1989) The great crash, the oil-Price shock and the unit-root hypothesis. Econometrica 57:1361–1401

Perron P (1990) Testing for a unit root in a time series with a changing mean. J Bus Econ Stat 8:153–162

Perron P (1997a) Further evidence on breaking trend functions in macroeconomic variables. J Econom 80(2):355–385

Perron P (1997b) L'estimation de Modèles avec Changements Structurels Multiples. L'Actual Econ 73(1):457–505

Perron P, Vogelsang TJ (1992) Nonstationarity and level shifts with an application to purchasing power parity. J Bus Econ Stat 10:301–320

Sansó A, Aragó V, Carrion-i-Silvestre JLl (2004) Testing for changes in the unconditional variance of financial time series. Revista Econ Financiera 4:32–53

Schaller H, Norden SV (1997) Regime switching in stock market returns. Appl Finan Econ 7(2):177-191

Tsay RS (1988) Outliers, level shifts and variance changes in time series. J Forecast 7:1–20

Valentinyi-Endrész M (2004) Structural breaks and financial risk management. MNB Working Papers 2004/11, Magyar Nemzeti Bank, The Central Bank of Hungary. http://english.mnb.hu/Root/Dokumentumtar/ENMNB/Kiadvanyok/mnben_mnbfuzetek/mnben_wp200411/wp2004_11v.pdf. Accessed 2 Jan 2009

Wilson B, Aggarwal R, Inclan C (1996) Detecting volatility changes across the oil sector. J Futur Mark 16:313–330

Zivot E, Andrews DWK (1992) Further evidence on the great crash, the oil price shock, and the unit-root hypothesis. J Bus Econ Stat 10:251–270

Chapter 3
Crises and Latent Structure in the Global Stock Market

We are in a minefield. No one knows where the mines are planted.

Atkins et al.

Abstract This chapter analyzes the stock market dynamics by exploring the latent structure in the global market, by classifying constituent markets in different categories. Once the structure is determined, the study attempts to answer a set of crucial and related questions namely, whether and how regional shocks lead to or transmit into global shock; in case of a purely regional shock, how do the regional markets behave? in case of a global shock, what is the nature of inter-regional and intra-regional stock market dynamics? And, finally, what is the source of volatility in these markets? The first stock market cycle has not been 'global' in true sense and was dominated by a single trend set by the combined group of the European and the American markets. The second phase was characterized by three distinct, dissociated structures. The European markets became the dominant group followed by the Asian and the American markets. Further presence of not so robust intra-regional associations offers immense scope for effective regional and global portfolio diversification. However, the fact that volatility has been consistently endogenous to each of these markets might warn us about the inherent instability of the global stock market.

Keywords Exploratory factor analysis · Dependence analysis · Granger causality · Latent structure · Stock market association · Portfolio diversification

3.1 Introduction

Analysts often argue that any regional crisis or any financial pandemic at any center cannot assume a fatal global dimension until and unless the peripheries are intrinsically vulnerable. Thus the financially viable and fundamentally stable peripheries

---

Quoted in Ralph Atkins, Michael Mackenzie and Paul J. Davies, "ECB Chief Fails to Reassure Markets", *Financial Times*, August 14, 2007.

G. Chakrabarti and C. Sen, *Anatomy of Global Stock Market Crashes*, SpringerBriefs in Economics, DOI: 10.1007/978-81-322-0463-3_3,

are most likely to remain dissociated from the crisis-centers and can avoid the heat of disaster. Roubini and Mihm (2010) however have found this so-called "decoupling thesis" loose-footed. Historically, financial diseases in any of the global financial centers have often been transmitted to other parts of the world leading ultimately to severe global epidemic: courtesy to the presence of many different channels of contagion. Contagions are, however, not by-product of recent global financial integration. It was realized and quiet appropriately stated by Baron Carl Meyer von Rothschild, as early as in 1875 that "the whole world has become a city" (Kindleberger 1978). Till then financial contagions have served as channels of spreading panic from one nation to others particularly during a period of crisis. Ignoring the contagions will make one miss the real essence of a crisis: the speed and simultaneity with which crises wreck anemic economies and shudder the healthy ones.

Our earlier analysis in Chap. 2 has hinted toward the possible presence of some inter-regional and intra-regional association in the global stock market under the different stock market cycles. However, to analyze the nature of such association in a bit detail, it is useful to start from an exploration of the possible latent structure in the global stock market. Researchers often use an exploratory factor analysis to reveal the latent structure of any system through classification of variables under different factors. This exercise could effectively be used in the context of analyzing stock market dynamics. Exploratory factor analysis can be used to explore the underlying structure of the global stock market by classification of constituent markets in different categories. Such market segmentation can be useful in analyzing the nature and the extent of financial integration in the global stock market. This chapter explores whether the stock markets all over the world form some 'group' among themselves around the two stock market cycles considered in the study. A comparison of the nature of latent structure around the two cycles could be of further interest.

Principal components and factor analyzes are useful multivariate techniques (Marascuilo and Levin 1983; Mardia et al. 1979) to study the contemporaneous co-movements and modeling of stock market returns (Meric and Meric 1989; Pilippatos et al. 1983; Meric et al. 2008; Kassim and Maiyastri 2004). Principal Component GARCH models are modified models for modeling of stock market returns (Alexander 2002). However, studies using principal component analysis and exploratory factor analysis in context of financial markets are limited.

3.2 Exploring the Latent Structure in the Global Stock Market

3.2.1 Methodology

The study uses daily stock return for each of the market indexes computed using the formula: $R_t = \ln(P_t/P_t - 1)$ over the study-period. The returns are then standardized.

The analysis is carried out for two sub-periods. The first phase, centered on the first cycle, considers the period from 1998 to 2005. The second sub-period ranges from 2006 to 2011 and is related to the second cycle.

Exploratory factor analysis (EFA) is a simple, non-parametric method for extracting relevant information from large correlated data sets (Hair et al. 2010). It could reduce a complex data set to a lower dimension to reveal the sometimes hidden, simplified structures that often underlie it. In EFA, each variable (X_i) is expressed as a linear combination of underlying factors (F_i). The amount of variance each variable shares with others is called communality. The covariance among variables is described by common factors and a unique factor (U_i) for each variable. Hence,

$$X_i = A_{i1}F_1 + \ldots\ldots + A_{im}F_m + V_iU_i \tag{3.1}$$

$$\text{and,}\quad F_i = W_{i1}X_1 + \ldots\ldots + W_{ik}X_k \tag{3.2}$$

where, A_{il} is the standardized multiple regression coefficient of variable i on factor j; V_i is the standardized regression coefficient of variable i on unique factor i; m is the number of common factors; W_i's are the factor scores and k is the number of variables. The unique factors are uncorrelated with each other and with common factors.

The appropriateness of using EFA on a data set could be judged by Bartlett's test of sphericity and the Kaiser-Meyar-Olkin (KMO) measure. The Bartlett's test of sphericity tests the null of population correlation matrix to be an identity matrix. A statistically significant Bartlett statistic indicates the extent of correlation among variables to be sufficient to use EFA. Moreover, Kaiser-Meyar-Olkin (KMO) measure of sampling adequacy should exceed 0.50 for appropriateness of EFA.

In factor analysis, the variables are grouped according to their correlation so that variables under a particular factor are strongly correlated with each other. When variables are correlated they will share variances among them. A variable's communality is the estimate of its shared variance among the variables represented by a specific factor.

Through appropriate methods, factor scores could be selected so that the first factor explains the largest portion of the total variance. Then a second set, uncorrelated to the first one, could be found so that the second factor accounts for most of the residual variance and so on. This chapter uses the principal component method where the total variance in data is considered. The method helps when we isolate minimum number of factors accounting for maximum variance in data.

Factors with eigenvalues greater than 1.0 are retained. An eigenvalue represents the amount of variance associated with the factor. Factors with eigenvalue less than 1 is no better than a single variable, because after standardization, each variable has a variance of 1.0.

Interpretation of factors will require an examination of the factor loadings. A factor loading is the correlation of the variable and the factor. Hence, the squared loading is the variable's total variance accounted by the factor. Thus a 0.50 loading implies that 25% of the variance of the variable is explained by the factor. Usually, factor loadings in the range of ±0.30 to ±0.40 are minimally required for interpretation of a structure. Loadings greater than or equal to ±0.50 are practically significant while loadings greater than or equal to ±0.70 imply presence of well-defined structures.

The initial or unrotated factor matrix, however, shows the relationship between the factors and the variables where factor solutions extract factors in the order of their variance extracted. The first factor accounting for the largest amount of variance in the data is a general factor where almost every variable has significant loading. The subsequent factors are based on the residual amount of variance. Such factors are difficult to interpret as a single factor could be related to many variables. Factor rotation provides simpler factor structures that are easier to interpret. With rotation, the reference axes of the factors are rotated about the origin, until some other positions are reached. With factor rotation variance is re-distributed from the earlier factor to the latter. Effectively, one factor will be significantly correlated with only a few variables and a single variable will have high and significant loading with only one factor. In an orthogonal factor rotation, as the axes are maintained at angles of 90°, the resultant factors will be uncorrelated to each other. Within the orthogonal factor rotation methods, VARIMAX is the most popular method where the sum of variances of the required loading of the factor matrix is maximized. There are however oblique factor rotations where the reference axes are not maintained at 90° angles. The resulting factors will not be totally uncorrelated to each other. This chapter will use that method of factor rotation which will fit the data best.

The study then employs Cronbach's alpha as a measure of internal consistency. In theory a high value of alpha is often used as evidence that the items measure an underlying (or latent) construct. Cronbach's alpha, however, is not a statistical test. It is a coefficient of reliability or consistency.

The standardized Cronbach's alpha could be written as: $a = \frac{N.\bar{c}}{\bar{v} + (N-1).\bar{c}}$

Here N is the number of items (here markets); $\bar{c}$ is the average inter-item covariance among the items and $\bar{v}$ is the average variance. From the formula, it is clear that an increase in the number of items increases Cronbach's alpha. Additionally, if the average inter-item correlation increases, Cronbach's alpha increases as well (holding the number of items constant). This study uses Cronbach's alpha to check how closely related a set of markets are as a group and whether they indeed form a 'group' among themselves.

Once the structures are identified, the study will explore the extent and nature of financial integration.

3.2.2 Result for Sub-Period 1 (1998–2005)

The analysis is carried out for those markets that experienced the first cycle.

Table 3.1 Communalities (phase 1)

	Initial	Extraction		Initial	Extraction
Brazil	1.000	0.468	Australia	1.000	0.598
Mexico	1.000	0.575	Hong Kong	1.000	0.672
Canada	1.000	0.799	Indonesia	1.000	0.477
Netherlands	1.000	0.673	Malaysia	1.000	0.612
Austria	1.000	0.454	Japan	1.000	0.624
Belgium	1.000	0.730	Argentina	1.000	0.758
France	1.000	0.863	DJ	1.000	0.838
Germany	1.000	0.802	NASDAQ	1.000	0.790
Switzerland	1.000	0.535	S&P	1.000	0.941
UK	1.000	0.788	Cairo	1.000	0.545

Extraction Method: Principal Component Analysis

a. KMO and Bartlett's Test

The Kaiser–Meyer–Olkin measure of sampling adequacy stands at 0.795 and Bartlett's test statistic is significant at 1% level of significance (approx. Chi-Square = 7865.114). These suggest appropriateness of applying EFA on the data set.

b. Communalities

Communalities as shown in Table 3.1 are sufficiently high for most of the markets. Thus shared variances are quite high for the markets concerned.

c. Factors retained and the latent structure

On the basis of eigenvalues, seven factors are extracted. The factors with the corresponding eigenvalues, their constituents and Cronbach's alpha are shown in Table 3.2.

As suggested by the Cronbach's alpha, there is only one valid structure in the market given by the first factor. This factor has an eigenvalue of 5.539 and could explain 27.7% of total market variability. This set of markets reflects the market trend during the first cycle. As is evident from the markets having strongest loading on the first factor, the factor reflects a strong association among the European and the US markets. No other valid regional structure could be found during this time period. Moreover, VARIMAX being the appropriate rotation method, the factors extracted are uncorrelated to each other. This implies presence of a single structure represented by a group of European and US group of markets that are completely dissociated from the other regions.

Table 3.2 Latent structure in global stock market (phase 1)

Factor	Eigenvalue (% of variance explained)	Markets (loadings)	Cronbach's alpha
1	5.539 (27.697)	Austria (0.509)	0.895
		Belgium (0.766)	
		France (0.864)	
		Germany (0.862)	
		Switzerland (0.579)	
		UK (0.823)	
		DJ (0.726)	
		NASDAQ (0.624)	
		S&P (0.745)	
2	2.049 (10.459)	Australia (0.478)	0.365
		Hong Kong (0.488)	
		Indonesia (0.409)	
3	1.556 (7.779)	Canada (0.696)	0.356
		Argentina (0.613)	
4	1.186 (5.928)	Cairo (0.542)	–
5	1.092 (5.460)	Mexico (−0.503)	−0.0038
		Netherlands (0.702)	
6	1.015 (5.074)	Malaysia (0.719)	–
7	1.006 (5.028)	Brazil (0.525)	0.0321
		Japan (0.606)	

3.2.3 Result for Sub-Period 2 (2006–2011)

a. KMO and Bartlett's Test

The Kaiser–Meyer–Olkin measure of sampling adequacy stands at 0.951 and Bartlett's test statistic is significant at 1% level of significance (approx. Chi-Square = 20250.4). These suggest appropriateness of applying EFA on the data set.

b. Communalities

Communalities for different markets for phase 2 are shown in Table 3.3.

The communalities are high in most of the markets except for Malaysia, China, Tel Aviv and Cairo. The common variances shared with other markets are thus sufficiently high for these markets.

c. Factors retained and the latent structure

The latent structure in the global stock market in phase 2 is shown in Table 3.4. Using the VARIMAX method of rotation, four factors are retained on the basis of eigenvalues. The market, however, is characterized by three uncorrelated structures. As is evident from the value of Cronbach's alpha, the fourth factor is not a valid structure. There is significant presence of regional integration. The European markets set the dominant trend in the market.

Table 3.3 Communalities (phase 2)

	Initial	Extraction		Initial	Extraction
Oslo	1.000	0.681	Malaysia	1.000	0.188
Spain	1.000	0.822	China	1.000	0.288
Netherlands	1.000	0.922	Seol	1.000	0.704
Austria	1.000	0.756	Japan	1.000	0.606
Belgium	1.000	0.859	Singapore	1.000	0.689
France	1.000	0.940	New Zealand	1.000	0.493
Germany	1.000	0.830	DJ	1.000	0.895
Stockholm	1.000	0.843	NASDAQ	1.000	0.896
Switzerland	1.000	0.823	S&P	1.000	0.926
UK	1.000	0.895	Brazil	1.000	0.775
Australia	1.000	0.629	Mexico	1.000	0.776
Hong Kong	1.000	0.758	Argentina	1.000	0.654
Indonesia	1.000	0.533	Canada	1.000	0.458
India	1.000	0.463	Cairo	1.000	0.189
Taiwan	1.000	0.619	Tel Aviv	1.000	0.301

Table 3.4 Latent structure in global stock market (phase 2)

Factor	Eigenvalue (% of variance explained)	Markets (loadings)	Cronbach's alpha
1	13.529 (45.096)	Norway (0.712)	0.975
		Austria (0.753)	
		Belgium (0.834)	
		France (0.899)	
		Germany (0.799)	
		Switzerland (0.833)	
		UK (0.876)	
		Spain (0.846)	
		Netherlands (0.883)	
		Stockholm (0.836)	
2	3.701 (12.337)	Australia (0.748)	0.893
		Hong Kong (0.820)	
		Indonesia (0.682)	
		India (0.551)	
		Taiwan (0.769)	
		Malaysia (0.383)	
		China (0.460)	
		Seol (0.812)	
		Japan (0.729)	
		Singapore (0.768)	
3	2.015 (6.718)	Dow Jones (0.886)	0.975
		NASDAQ (0.892)	
		S&P (0.903)	
		Brazil (0.801)	
		Mexico (0.778)	
		Argentina (0.683)	
4	1.064 (3.546)	New Zealand (0.700)	0.109
		Canada (0.671)	

The eigenvalue of the first factor in the second phase is much higher than that in the first one reflecting a stronger market trend. The Asian market has been the second important factor, while the American markets are clubbed under the third factor. These two factors have been of much less importance than the first one as is reflected by their respective eigenvalues. The internal consistency and individual loadings, however, have been much higher in the second phase. Hence, the extent of regional association has been stronger in the second phase. The three regions, however, have been completely dissociated from each other. The markets of Tel Aviv and Cairo are excluded from this analysis as they possess insignificant factor loadings.

It now remains to explore the extent and nature of financial integration in each of these regions isolated by the exploratory factor analysis. The first phase is characterized to be single dominant trend coming from the European and US markets in a combined manner. There is no distinct regional association. The second phase, however, is characterized by three distinct structures. Although the European markets have been the dominant, the Asian and American (both North and South) markets have distinct roles to play and most interestingly, there has been no inter-regional association.

3.3 Analysis of Intra-Regional Association

The nature of intra-regional association will be analyzed in two ways. Firstly, the study will seek to explore the possible presence of lead-lag relationship within each region. Secondly, it will attempt to isolate the role of each market in explaining the variance of other market returns. In this way, the study will analyze the return movement associations and volatility movement associations, if any, in the global stock market.

3.3.1 Methodology: Granger Causality

Globalization and growing financial integration have invoked inquiries into stock market co-movements. In the early literature, stock market associations are found to strengthen with global financial integration (Agmon 1972; Hilliard 1979) and to disappear for isolated financial markets (Ripley 1973). The 1987 crash of the US market has strengthened co-movement of stock price indices (Arshanapalli and Doukas 1993). Cheung and Ng (1992) showed the same result for the period 1985–1989. Eun and Shim (1989) reinforced the finding using a VAR model and impulse response function. Lee and Kim (1994) cited evidence for a significant increase in the association of the stock price indices after the crash. Jeon and Von-Furstenberg (1990) arrived at the same conclusion applying the VAR approach and the impulse response function analysis. Koch and Koch (1991) used dynamic simultaneous equations to obtain the result that the markets are getting increasingly interdependent. Masih and Masih (1997a, b, 2001) performed the cointegration test to prove the interdependency among the Asian market and the dominant influence of the US and the UK. Koutmos (1996) used multivariate VAR-EGARCH model to conclude that there is interdependency among the European markets. Financial market interlinkage often results in a shock spillover showed the presence of contagion in Asian financial markets. Glezakos et al. (2007) examined the short and long-run interlinkages between major world financial markets with particular attention to the Greek stock exchange. They have found strong influence of the US financial market, DAX and FTSE on the other markets of the sample. Moreover, sectoral indices, particularly the IT indices are related globally. NASDAQ-100, for example, could be shown to be the major origin for the shocks in the IT.CAC and the NEMAX with the help of a VAR model with GARCH errors (Suleimann 2003a, b). Sharma and Kennedy (1977) find strong link between the Indian, US and UK markets. Rao and Naik (1990) conducted a cross-spectral analysis to trace a weak relationship between the Indian market with international markets during the controlled Indian economy regime. In recent years, Wong et al. (2005) have tried to identify the volatility transmission channels for the Indian stock market.

The vector autoregression (VAR) is commonly used for the forecasting systems of interrelated time series and for analyzing the dynamic impact of random disturbances on the system of variables. The VAR approach sidesteps the need for structural modeling by modeling every endogenous variable in the system as a function of the lagged values of all of the endogenous variables in the system. The model could be described as:

$$Y_t = A_1 Y_{t-1} + \ldots\ldots + A_p Y_{t-p} + BX_t + \varepsilon_t \tag{3.3}$$

Y_t: k vector of endogenous variables, X_t: d vector of exogenous variables, $A_1,\ldots,A_p$, B: matrices of coefficients to be estimated, ε_t: innovations vector that may be contemporaneously correlated with each other but are uncorrelated with their own lagged values and uncorrelated with all of the right-hand side variables. Since only lagged values of the endogenous variables appear on the right-hand side of each equation, there is no issue of simultaneity, and OLS is the appropriate estimation technique. However, the assumption that the disturbances are not serially correlated is not restrictive because any serial correlation could be absorbed by adding more lagged y's. The appropriate lag length is chosen on the basis of Akaike information criteria, the Schwartz information criteria and the likelihood ratio test.

Granger (1969) tried to explore the issue of whether x causes y, to see how much of the current y can be explained by past values of y and then to see whether adding lagged values of x can improve the explanation. For any two x and y, y is said to be Granger-caused by x if x helps in the prediction of y, or equivalently if the coefficients on the lagged x's are statistically significant. However, the statement "x Granger causes y" does not necessarily imply that y is the effect or the result of x. Granger causality measures precedence but does not by itself indicate causality in the more common use of the term.

3.3.2 Methodology: Dependence Analysis

Within each factor, the study will explore whether and how a market's variance could be explained by the other markets within that group. The study will make use of a simple multiple regression technique and that is permissible as the study works with stationary return series. In this analysis, we work with a set of independent variables that are closely associated with each other (since they belong to the same factor). If the independent variables are correlated, they would share their predictive power. Instead of working with the multiple-correlation-coefficient, this study makes use of part or semi-partial correlation coefficient. According to Hair et al. (2010), the part correlation gives us the unique relationship predicted by an independent variable after the predictions shared with all other independent variables are removed. The squared part correlation thus represents the unique variance explained by a particular explanatory variable. In this study, part correlations will be used to explore the unique variance explained by different markets.

3.3.3 Results for Phase 1

3.3.3.1 Results for Applying Granger Causality

Table 3.5 shows the lead-lag relationship among the nine markets that constitute the only valid construct in the world market. The US markets are not characterized by any lead-lag relationship among them. This is not surprising as perhaps these markets moved simultaneously during the first cycle. There is some lead-lag relationship among the European and the US markets. While Dow Jones leads Austrian market, there are both-way relationships among Dow Jones and other European markets. So far as the two other US markets are concerned, NASDAQ and S&P lead all the European markets except for Switzerland.

3.3.3.2 Results for Applying Dependence Techniques

Table 3.6 shows the unique variance of a market return explained by other markets that belong to the same group. As is evident from the table, the markets, even if they belong to the same group, can individually explain only a small portion of the other markets' return variance. Hence, variability in a particular market can hardly be attributed to the variability of the other markets with which it is associated. The unique variance explained by the US markets however has been comparatively higher in case of other US markets.

Table 3.5 Results for applying Granger causality (phase 1)

	Leads	Lags	Both way	No lead-lag relation
Austria	Switzerland[a]	Germany[a], Dow Jones[a] NASDAQ[a] S&P[a]	–	Belgium France UK
Belgium	UK[a] Switzerland[a]	NASDAQ[a] S&P[a]	Germany[a] Dow Jones[a]	Austria, France
Germany	Austria[aa] UK[a]	NASDAQ[a] S&P[a]	Belgium[a] Dow Jones[a] France[a] Switzerland[a]	–
France	Switzerland[a]	NASDAQ[a] S&P[a]	Germany[a] Dow Jones[a]	Austria Belgium UK
UK	Switzerland[a]	Belgium[a] Germany[a] NASDAQ[a] S&P[a]	Dow Jones[a]	Austria France
Switzerland	–	Austria[a] Belgium[a] France[a] UK[a]	Germany[a] Dow Jones[a] NASDAQ[a] S&P[a]	–
Dow Jones	Austria[a]	–	France[a] Belgium[a] Germany[a] UK[a] Switzerland[a]	NASDAQ S&P
NASDAQ	Austria[a] Belgium[a] Germany[a] France[a] UK[a]	–	Switzerland[a]	S&P Dow Jones
S&P	Austria[a] Belgium[a] Germany[a] France[a] UK[a]	–	Switzerland[a]	NASDAQ Dow Jones

[a] implies significance at 1% level

3.3.4 Results for Phase 2

As suggested by the exploratory factor analysis, there were three valid constructs during phase 2. The first construct has been the European markets constituted of the markets of Norway, Austria, Belgium, France, Germany, Switzerland, UK, Spain, Netherlands and Stockholm. The second construct has been the Asia–Pacific region constituted of the markets of Australia, Hong Kong, Indonesia,

Table 3.6 Unique variance of a market return explained by other markets (phase 1) (in percentage)

	Independent variables								
	Austria	Belgium	France	Germany	Switzerland	UK	DJ	S&P	NASDAQ
Austria	–	0.60	0.09	0.26	0.28	0.10	0.06	0.04	0.04
Belgium	1.0	–	1.17	0.12	2.62	0.53	0.001	0.01	0.30
France	3.8	3.00	–	6.81	0.36	8.01	0.01	0.00	0.04
Germany	0.80	0.20	4.80	–	0.00	0.37	0.03	0.00	0.18
Switzerland	0.40	2.00	0.21	0.28	–	0.17	0.00	0.00	0.09
UK	0.30	0.80	5.11	0.34	0.29	–	0.0049	0.01	0.02
DJ	0.50	0.004	0.01	0.10	0.03	0.02	–	19.62	7.34
S&P	0.20	0.20	0.03	0.24	0.72	0.03	35.88	–	27.67
NASDAQ	0.60	0.10	0.0004	0.0003	0.67	0.04	3.10	6.35	–

India, Taiwan, Malaysia, China, Seoul, Japan and Singapore. The third valid construct incorporates the American markets, namely, the US, Brazil, Mexico and Argentina. Intra-regional associations will now be explored using the Granger causality and dependency technique for each construct separately.

3.3.4.1 Results for Applying Granger Causality

Table 3.7 reveals intra-regional associations within the European region. The stock market of Norway has almost no lead-lag relationship with the other European markets, except for Austria that lags Norway. The same is the case for the Stockholm stock market. Specifically, the region is mostly characterized by the absence of lead-lag relationship among the markets. Some both-way causality, however, could be found in some of these markets. The stock market of Germany has both-way connection with five other markets. The Swiss market is also connected by both-way relationship with four markets. Austria and Belgium lag three markets each. Except for Germany and UK, each of the other stock markets leads any one of the other markets.

As is suggested from the Table 3.8, the Asian region is characterized by presence of some lead-lag relationship. Both-way relationship is however not very dominant in this region. The Indian market lags none and leads all but two markets in the region. Indonesia leads six other markets and follows only the Indian market. Australia leads none and lags four. Hong Kong leads four and follows three other markets. China leads three and follows two. While Singapore followed none, Malaysia has been mostly a follower. The presence of intra-regional association, however, has been stronger in the Asian region than the European region considered earlier.

The association within the American region (construct 3) has been depicted in Table 3.9.

This region, like the European one, is mostly characterized by the absence of lead-lag relationship. The Brazilian market has no lead-lag relationship with the

Table 3.7 Results for applying Granger causality (phase 2, factor 1)

	Leads	Lags	Both way	No lead-lag relation
Austria	UK[a]	Netherlands[a] Norway[a] Stockholm[a]	Germany[a]	Belgium, France Spain, Switzerland
Belgium	Austria[a]	France[a] Spain[a] Switzerland[a]	–	Germany, Netherlands, Norway, Stockholm, UK
France	Belgium[a]	Switzerland[a]	Germany[a]	Austria, Netherlands Norway, Spain, Stockholm, UK
Germany	–	Spain[a]	Austria[a], France[a] Netherlands[a] Switzerland[a]UK[a]	Belgium, Norway Stockholm
Netherlands	Austria[a]	–	Germany[a] Switzerland[a]	Belgium, France UK, Spain, Norway Stockholm
Norway	Austria[a]	–	–	Belgium, France Germany, Netherlands, Spain Stockholm, Switzerland, UK
Spain	Belgium[a] Germany[a]	–	–	Austria, France, Netherlands, Norway Stockholm, Switzerland, UK
Stockholm	Austria[a]	–	–	Belgium, France Germany, Netherlands, Norway, Spain, Switzerland, UK
Switzerland	Belgium[a]	–	France[a] Germany[a] Netherlands[a] UK[a]	Austria, Norway, Spain, Stockholm
UK	–	Austria[a]	Germany[a] Switzerland[a]	Belgium, France, Spain, Netherlands, Norway, Stockholm

[a] implies significance at 1% level

others. Within the Latin American region some relationship could be found only between the Mexican and the Argentinean markets. Within the US market, all the three indexes are not connected by lead-lag relationship. While NASDAQ is connected to both DJ30 and S&P, the two latter markets are not connected with each other by any lead-lag relationship.

3.3.4.2 Results for Applying Dependency Techniques

The part correlations are calculated for all the markets within each of the three constructs. Table 3.10 shows the percentage of variance of any European market return that could be explained by the other markets within the same construct. As the results suggest, percentage of variance of market return explained uniquely by

Table 3.8 Results for applying Granger causality (phase 2, factor 2)

	Leads	Lags	Both way	No lead-lag relation
Australia	–	Hong Kong[a] India[a] Indonesia[a] Singapore[a]	Malaysia[a]	China, Japan, Seoul, Taiwan
China	Hong Kong[a] Japan[a] Seoul[a]	India[a] Indonesia[a]	–	Australia, China, Malaysia, Singapore
Hong Kong	Australia[a] Malaysia[a] Seoul[a] Taiwan[a]	China[a] India[a] Indonesia[a]	Japan[a] Singapore[a]	–
India	Australia[a] China[a] Hong Kong[a] Indonesia[a] Japan[a] Malaysia[a] Taiwan[a]	–	Seoul[a]	Singapore
Indonesia	Australia[a] China[a] Hong Kong[a] Japan[a] Malaysia[a] Seoul[a]	India[a]	Taiwan[a]	Singapore
Japan	Malaysia[a] Seoul[a]	China[a] India[a] Indonesia[a] Singapore[a]	Hong Kong[a]	Australia, Taiwan

(continued)

Table 3.8 (continued)

	Leads	Lags	Both way	No lead-lag relation
Malaysia	–	India[a] Indonesia[a] Hong Kong[a] Japan[a] Seoul[a] Singapore[a] Taiwan[a]	Australia[a]	China
Seoul	Malaysia[a]	China[a] Hong Kong[a] Indonesia[a] Japan[a] Singapore[a]	India[a]	Australia, Taiwan
Singapore	Australia[a] Japan[a] Malaysia[a] Seoul[a]	–	Taiwan[a] Hong Kong[a]	China, India, Indonesia
Taiwan	Malaysia[a]	Hong Kong[a] India[a]	Singapore[a] Indonesia[a]	Australia, China, Japan, Seoul

[a] implies significance at 1% level

Table 3.9 Results for applying Granger causality (phase 2, factor 3)

	Leads	Lags	Both way	No lead-lag relation
Argentina	–	Mexico[a], NASDAQ[a]	–	Brazil, DJ30, S&P
Brazil	–	–	–	Mexico, Argentina, DJ30, S&P, NASDAQ
Mexico	Argentina[a]	–	DJ30[a], S&P[a]	Brazil, NASDAQ
DJ30	NASDAQ[a]	–	Mexico[a]	Argentina, Brazil, S&P
S&P	–	–	Mexico[a] NASDAQ[a]	Brazil, Argentina, DJ30
NASDAQ	Argentina[a]	DJ30[a]	S&P[a]	Brazil, Mexico

[a] implies significance at 1% level

Table 3.10 Unique variance of a market return explained by other markets (in%) (phase 2, factor 1)

	Independent variable									
	Norway	Spain	Netherlands	Austria	Belgium	France	Germany	Stockholm	Switzerland	UK
Norway	–	0.001	1.04	2.4	0.18	0.18	0.004	1.61	0.16	1.19
Spain	0.0004	–	0.1	0.3	0.3	3.5	0.01	0.1	0.01	0.04
Netherlands	0.25	0.02	–	0.01	0.64	1.3	0.06	0.02	0.003	0.31
Austria	2.07	0.38	0.04	–	0.56	0.01	0.12	1.00	0.18	0.02
Belgium	0.10	0.26	1.49	0.37	–	0.22	0.07	0.07	0.19	0.04
France	0.03	0.85	0.74	0.002	0.05	–	0.76	0.04	0.13	0.50
Germany	0.0001	0.01	0.10	0.058	0.06	2.34	–	0.28	0.04	0.03
Stockholm	0.96	0.07	0.05	0.69	0.08	0.18	0.38	–	0.05	0.04
Switzerland	0.10	0.01	0.01	0.13	0.21	0.56	0.05	0.05	–	1.04
UK	0.36	0.02	0.41	0.01	0.02	1.10	0.02	0.02	0.53	–

any market has been almost negligible for each of the markets. Hence, volatility in any of the European markets could hardly be explained by the movements in the other European markets.

Table 3.11 shows whether and how the volatility in any Asian market could be explained solely by other markets in the region.

The percentage of variation in any market return explained solely by each of the other markets has remained negligible. In most of the cases the percentage has been less than one. There are, however, some exceptions. Japan and Australia could explain near about 6% of variability in each other's market return. Similarly, Hong Kong and Singapore could explain nearly 7% of volatility in each other. Hong Kong could explain 8% of the Chinese market variability. However, in these cases, a large portion of variability in each of these markets remains unexplained by the variability in the region.

Table 3.12 shows the percentage of variance of any American market return that could be explained by the other markets within the same construct.

As is evident from the results, percentage of return variance of any market can hardly be explained uniquely by the other markets within the same construct. However, a closer look at Table 3.12 could reveal some interesting result. Within the US region, S&P could uniquely explain 9.73 and 4.28% of the return variance of DJ30 and NASDAQ, respectively. Moreover, DJ30 could explain 5.86% of volatility in S&P index. Within the Latin American markets Argentina and Mexico could respectively explain 5.2 and 6.15% of volatility in the Brazilian market. Brazil could explain 6.66 and 7.51% of volatility in the Mexican and Argentinean markets. Thus, within the American market construct, the US markets and the Latin American markets are related among themselves in terms of volatility transmission from the respective region. However, even for these markets, a large portion of variability remains unexplained.

3.4 The Latent Structure and the New Issues Arising

The study thus far has revealed significant results regarding the latent structure and inter-regional and intra-regional associations in the global stock markets. The nature of the global stock market movement has been significantly different during the two stock market cycles in the study. The first stock market cycle was not the 'global' in true sense as it affected only a limited number of markets. The market was dominated by a single trend where the European and the American markets remained the significant players. These markets were capable of explaining 28% of the total market variability. The second cycle however was truly global in nature. The latent structure during this period has been quite different from the first one. The second phase is characterized by three distinct structures. The European markets exclusively have been the dominant group in the global market explaining almost 45% of global variability. The Asian markets have now some role to play in the global market where they can explain 12% of the total variability.

Table 3.11 Unique variance of a market return explained by other markets (in %) (phase 2, factor 2)

	Independent variable									
	Australia	Hong Kong	Indonesia	India	Taiwan	Malaysia	China	Seoul	Japan	Singapore
Australia	–	0.53	0.30	0.002	1.12	0.17	0.03	0.37	5.90	0.11
Hong Kong	0.35	–	0.04	0.67	0.06	0.02	2.66	0.55	0.50	7.18
Indonesia	0.38	0.07	–	1.23	0.36	1.21	0.00	0.38	0.03	2.43
India	0.002	1.49	1.37	–	0.01	0.02	0.04	0.09	0.22	3.39
Taiwan	1.14	0.10	0.29	0.005	–	0.10	0.04	5.95	0.12	0.35
Malaysia	0.32	0.07	1.82	0.02	0.18	–	0.71	0.12	0.09	0.49
China	0.06	7.95	0.004	0.06	0.08	0.72	–	0.001	0.03	0.44
Seoul	0.30	0.69	0.24	0.05	4.80	0.05	0.0004	–	2.69	0.13
Japan	5.90	0.77	0.02	0.15	0.12	0.04	0.01	3.28	–	0.06
Singapore	0.08	7.73	1.35	1.66	0.24	0.18	0.16	0.11	0.04	–

Table 3.12 Unique variance of a market return explained by other markets (in %) (phase 2, factor 3)

	Independent variable					
	DJ30	NASDAQ	S&P	Brazil	Mexico	Argentina
DJ30	–	0.12	9.73	0.004	0.0004	0.07
NASDAQ	0.32	–	4.28	0.006	0.10	0.05
S&P	5.86	0.98	–	0.008	0.001	0.07
Brazil	0.04	0.03	0.14	–	6.15	5.20
Mexico	0.01	0.41	0.02	6.66	–	0.52
Argentina	1.02	0.29	1.69	7.51	0.69	–

The American markets, on the contrary, have lost their dominance and could explain only 7% of the global variability. The three regions, however, are completely dissociated from each other. A detailed analysis of intra-regional associations shows presence of some lead-lag relationship among the markets concerned. Over the first phase of study, the US markets were not characterized by any lead-lag relationship among them. However, there has been some lead-lag relationship among the European and the US markets. During the second phase, the European and the American regions have been mostly characterized by an absence of strong lead-lag relationship. The presence of intra-regional association, however, has been stronger in the Asian region. However, the markets, even if they belong to the same group, can individually explain only a small portion of the other markets' return variance. Hence, variability in a particular market can hardly be attributed to the variability of the other markets with which it is associated. This is a common trend prevailing in both the periods.

The findings could have significant implications for the global investors. There is immense scope for effective portfolio diversification in the global market. A global portfolio with stocks from different regions might reduce risks significantly. A regional portfolio construction might even be beneficial if the stocks from 'non-associated' markets could be selected. The investors, however, should take decisions cautiously. In recent years, the European region being the prime determinant of global variability might be a risky place for investment. Investments in the Asian and particularly in the American markets might be particularly beneficial for the investors. The absence of volatility transmission from other markets might make the investors feel more secured.

The last issue, however, should not be taken lightly as this might lead to some serious problems at the investment as well as the policy level. The fact that the volatility in any of the markets is not explained by the other markets with which it is associated might make a researcher inquisitive about the possible source of volatility in the global stock market. More specifically, these findings lead us to the possibility of the volatility being largely endogenous. Rather than originating from another stock market, volatility, stock market cycles and crashes might well be manifestations of the inherent instability or at best, of the knife-edge stability of any market. Fluctuations might be self-generating and endogenous to the system, rather than aberration and markets might be characterized by non-periodic limit cycles. Hence, no external shock will be required to gear financial crisis at regular intervals which, in an integrated financial world, will reverberate across the globe in no time. The fact that a stock market is chaotic has significant economic and policy implications. A chaotic stock market invalidates the assumption of efficient market. With efficient market hypothesis on trial, some investment strategies that were discarded earlier might now appear to be proficient. Policy prescriptions, based on the presumption of linearity, however, are likely to be ineffective when applied on a system which is actually nonlinear. Moreover, long-term economic forecasting is no longer feasible. At the theoretical level, a chaotic financial market suggests reorientation of traditional asset pricing models as the supporting pillar of these models namely, the Gaussian assumption about probability distribution seems to break down in a chaotic framework.

It is particularly this consideration that has led the study to explore the possible chaotic nature of the global stock markets in the next chapter.

References

Agmon T (1972) The relations among equity markets: a study of share price co-movements in the United States, United Kingdom, Germany and Japan. J Finan 27(4):839–855

Alexander CO (2002) Principal component models for generating large GARCH covariance matrices. Econ Notes 31(2):337–359

Arshanapalli B, Doukas J (1993) International stock market linkages: evidence from the pre- and post-October 1987 period. J Banking Finan 17:193–208

Bang Jeon, Von Furstenberg (1990) Growing international co-movement in stock price indexes. Quart Rev Econ Finan 30(30):17–30

Cheung YW, Ng LK (1992) Stock price dynamics and firm size: an empirical investigation. J Finan 47:1985–1997

Eun C, Shim S (1989) International transmission of stock market movements. J Finan Quant Anal 24:241–256

Glezakos M, Merika A, Kaligosfiris H (2007) Interdependence of major world stock exchanges: how is the Athens stock exchange affected? Int Res J Finan Econ 7:24–39

Granger CWJ (1969) Investigating causal relations by econometric models and cross-spectral methods. Econometrica 37(3):424–438

Hair JF, Black WC, Babin BJ, Anderson R (2010) Multivariate data analysis, 7th edn. Prentice Hall, Upper Saddle River, New Jersey

Hilliard J (1979) The relationship between equity indices on world exchanges. J Finan March 34(1):103–114

Kassim H, Maiyastri (2004) Principal component analysis in modelling stock market returns. Matematika 20(1):31–41

Kindleberger CP (1978) Manias, panics and crashes: a history of financial crises. Basic Books, New York

Koch PD, Koch TW (1991) Evolution in dynamic linkages across daily national stock indexes. J Int Money Finan 10:231–251

Koutmos G (1996) Modeling the dynamic interdependence of major European stock markets. J Bus Finan Account 23(7):975–988

Lee SB, Kim KJ (1994) Does the October 1987 crash strengthen the co-movement in stock price indexes. Quart Rev Econ Bus 3(1–2):89–102

Marascuilo LA, Levin JR (1983) Multivariate statistics in the social sciences: a researcher's guide. Brooks/Cole Publishing Company, Monterey

Mardia K, Kent J, Bibby J (1979) Multivariate analysis. Academy, New York

Masih AMM, Masih R (1997a) A comparative analysis of the propagation of stock market fluctuations in alternative models of dynamic causal linkages. Appl Finan Econ 7(1):59–74

Masih AMM, Masih R (1997b) Dynamic linkages and the propagation mechanism driving major international stock markets: an analysis of the pre- and post-crash eras. Quart Rev Econ Finan 37(4):859–885

Masih R, Masih AMM (2001) Long and short-term dynamic causal transmission amongst international stock markets. J Int Money Finan 20:563–587

Meric I, Meric G (1989) Potential gains from inter-temporal portfolio diversification and inter-temporal stability and seasonality in international stock market relationships. J Banking Finance 13(4/5): 627–640

Meric I, Kim S, Kim JH, Meric G (2008) Co-movements of U.S., U.K., and Asian stock markets before and after September 11, 2001. J Money Invest Bank 3:47–57

Philippatos GC, Christofi A, Christofi P (1983) The inter-temporal stability of international stock market relationships: another view. Finan Manage 12(4):63–69

Rao BSR, Naik U (1990) Inter-relatedness of stock market spectral investigation of USA, Japan and Indian markets note. Artha Vignana 32(3–4):309–321

Ripley D (1973) Systematic elements in the linkage of national stock market indices. Rev Econ Statist 55:356–361

Roubini N, Mihm S (2010) Crisis economics. Allen Lane Penguin Books, London

Sharma JL, Kennedy RE (1977) Comparative analysis of stock price behavior on the Bombay, London and New York stock exchanges. J Finan Quant Anal Sept 12(3):391–403

Suleimann R (2003a) Should stock market indexes time varying correlations be taken into account? a conditional variance multivariate approach. http://ideas.repec.org/p/wpa/wuwpwm/0307004.html. Accessed 16 Mar 2007

Suleimann R (2003b) The contagion effect between the volatilities of the NASDAQ-100 and the IT.CAC: a univariate and a bivariate switching approach. http://ideas.repec.org/p/wpa/wuwpwm/0307002.html. Accessed 16 Mar 2007

Wong WK, Agarwal A, Jun D (2005) Financial integration for Indian stock market, a fractional cointegration approach. Departmental working paper no. wp0501, Department of economics, National University of Singapore. http://nt2.fas.nus.edu.sg/ecs/pub/wp/wp0501.pdf. Accessed 19 Aug 2006

Chapter 4
Global Stock Market, Knife-Edge Stability and the Crisis

You believe in a God who plays dice, and I in complete law and order..,

Albert Einstein

Abstract This chapter explores whether the global markets are intrinsically unstable following the line of a growing body of the literature and inquires the possible nonlinear, particularly chaotic nature of these markets. The study finds all the markets to be deterministic. While over the first cycle nineteen markets were chaotic, the number increases to twenty four during the second one. Thus stock markets are inherently unstable; or are, at best, stable on knife-edge. Cycles and crashes are manifestations of this inherent instability: norms rather than aberrations. There is no determinate equilibrium and no external shock will be required to gear financial crisis at regular intervals which, in an integrated financial world, will reverberate across the globe in no time. The findings have significant theoretical and policy implications. The relevant equations of motion underlying the nonlinear global stock market return, no doubt can be determined, but it would be nearly impossible to forecast beyond a short time frame. Policy prescriptions, based on the presumption of linearity are likely to be ineffective when applied on a system which is actually nonlinear. At the theoretical level, a chaotic stock market puts efficient market hypothesis on trial and requires reframing of traditional asset pricing models.

Keywords Non-linearity · Chaos · Determinism · Knife-edge stability · False nearest neighborhood · Mutual information criterion · Maximum Lyapunov exponent

4.1 Introduction

The three most important revolutions in the field of science in twentieth century has been the theory of relativity, the theory of quantum mechanics and the chaos theory. The first two theories rely a lot upon calculus, which again stands on the premise of

---

Albert Einstein, Letter to Max Born, September 1944.

G. Chakrabarti and C. Sen, *Anatomy of Global Stock Market Crashes*, SpringerBriefs in Economics, DOI: 10.1007/978-81-322-0463-3_4,

simple linear approximations of nonlinear behavior. But chaos theory is different from the first two in the sense it deals with nonlinear behavior of a system. A chaotic system is essentially nonlinear; the time-dependent variables share a nonlinear relation. Assuming a system to be linear often resorts to some oversimplifications which are invalid in a real world. It is like solving a physics problem assuming no friction and no wind resistance. However, "In the real world, however, friction cannot be ignored and wind is blowing from all direction" (Baranger 2001).

At the beginning, chaos started as a mere mathematical curiosity and any random or irregular behavior in the related system were treated as anomalies. But the next three decades saw an ever increasing interest in this topic, which eventually revolutionized the way things were being perceived. Chaotic behavior is observed in chemical reactions, astronomy, molecular vibrations, combustion, cardiology, robotic systems, financial analysis, population growth and weather forecasting to name a few. The length of Britain's coastline follows a chaotic pattern. Even in 1993, Goldstar & Co. created a washing machine using chaos theory! Chaos, to be precise surrounds us. Most of the natural phenomena are chaotic in nature. This concept has revolutionized the way scientists treat various systems as it gave them freedom to look at the more complex nonlinear dynamics. However, Stewart (2002) objects to the term "non-linear dynamics". According to him dynamics are nonlinear in nature. So far the scientists were busy interpreting systems in the light of linearity. So if they stumble upon something which does not fit their perception and christen it nonlinear that would be ridiculous. It would be like naming the study of animals "non-elephantine zoology" if suddenly humans discover that there are millions of other species in the ecosystem other than elephants.

For a system to be chaotic, it must be *nonlinear*, *deterministic* and *sensitive to initial condition*. A linear system is never chaotic. Moreover, although it sounds perplexing, a chaotic system is deterministic rather than probabilistic. Future states of a chaotic system depend on some underlying rules. Finally, a chaotic system is sensitive to initial conditions unlike linear and stochastic systems, where as iterations increase, the error in the system increases proportionally. So in a stochastic system, a small error always remains a small error. This is not the case with a nonlinear chaotic system. A minuscule change in the initial condition can generate an error that increases exponentially with every iteration and eventually grows beyond 100% after only a few iterations. An example of a billiard table can be drawn here. If the system is stochastic, given the angle of the hit and position of the balls on the board, it is possible to know the position of the balls at any given point of time. But, in reality, the system is actually nonlinear and chaotic as a very small change in the angle of the hit (as small as an error at the 21st decimal place) will generate an error in prediction so big that after only a small number of iterations, if the position of the ball has to be predicted, it will be outside the billiard table. Another real life example of the sensitive dependence was what Edward Lorenz faced in 1963. He found a drastic change in the climatic prediction if the data is rounded off even slightly. A popular theory based on the premise of sensitive dependence on initial condition (SDIC) is the *Butterfly Effect*. It says that the flutter of the wings of a butterfly in Mexico can cause or stop a tornado in New

York. So at the end of the day it is the initial condition that matters the most. Because of the sensitive dependence, long run prediction cannot be made.

The variables in a chaotic system are functions of time. So the system continues to change with time. All possible values of the variables are called the "state space". And the path the system travels with time is known as the trajectory or orbit. Given the initial condition, to solve the system, one has to find this trajectory. The sensitivity to initial condition ensures that initially two very close points on two different trajectories will eventually diverge from each other in an exponential rate.

Another important characteristic of chaotic systems is there must be a hidden order in the chaos. Feignenbaum pointed out that a single stable state continues to split into two periodical stable states at a universally constant rate of 4.66920.

The history of chaos dates back to 1890 when Henri Poincaré won the prize by King Oscar II of Sweden, for coming closest to solve the n-body problem. While proving the instability of the solar system for more than three celestial bodies he threw the first light on the complex nature of nonlinear system. Hadamard (1898) first pointed out the importance of sensitivity to initial condition, which was farther supported by Poincaré in 1903 "....it may happen that small differences in the initial conditions produce very great ones in the final phenomena. A small error in the former will produce a large one in the latter. Prediction becomes impossible". The chaos was born, but yet unnamed until Tien-Yien Li and James Yorke introduced the term "chaos theory" in their 1975 paper "Period Three Implies Chaos".

Benoit Mandelbrot introduced the mathematics of fractals in 1975 which brought an end to reductionism. Fractals are geometric shapes which are chaotic in space. Fractals are self-similar, that means, they do not become simpler when magnified to any level. In 1971, David Ruelle and Floris Takens introduced the concept of strange attractors, which is a fractal generating technique. Attractors are the set of motion to which a dynamic system evolves in the long run. A chaotic system exhibits strange attractor.

A majority of studies in deterministic chaos use tests for estimating the fractal dimension, mainly the Grassberger and Procaccia (1983) algorithm. Information about the fractal dimension helps understand the underlying attractor. The GP algorithm estimates the fractal dimension as the correlation dimension (D). D is calculated as the slope of the log–log plot of C_m (the correlation integral) and ε (radius). However, as Theiler pointed out, if the data is nonstationary and has time-dependent noise, the GP algorithm based on the correlation integral is no longer effective. Theiler (1986) suggested a slight redefining of the correlation integral in that case (known as the Theiler correction).

4.2 Methodology

The methodology is described in the following few sub-sections. It has been however, the same as that we have used in some of our earlier studies (Chakrabarti 2010a, 2010a; Chakrabarti et al. 2010; Sen et al. 2011).

4.2.1 BDS Test

For a time series to be deterministic and chaotic, it has to be nonlinear at first. Therefore, it is necessary to check for non-linearity in the underlying series. For this, the BDS test, named after Brock, Dechert and Scheinkman is used. The test developed by Brock et al. (1996) is a popular test for non-linearity. It was initially used to test for the null hypothesis of independent and identical distribution (IID) for the purpose of detecting non-random chaotic dynamics. However, BDS test has power against a wide range of linear and nonlinear alternatives (Brock et al. 1991; Barnett et al. 1997). The test can also be used as a portmanteau test or mis-specification test when applied to the residuals from a fitted model, particularly a linear time series model.

To perform the test, a distance ε is first chosen. If the observations of the series are IID, then for any pair of points, the probability of the distance between these points being less than or equal to epsilon, $c_1(\varepsilon)$, will be constant. A set consisting of multiple pairs of points is now chosen by moving through the consecutive observations of the sample in order. That is, given an observation s, and an observation t of a series X, a set of pairs of the following form can be constructed:

$$\{\{X_s, X_t\}, \{X_{s+1}, X_{t+1}\}, \{X_{s+2}, X_{t+2}\}, \ldots, \{X_{s+m-1}, X_{t+m-1}\}\}$$

where m is the number of consecutive points used in the set, or embedding dimension. The joint probability of every pair of points in the set satisfying the epsilon condition by the probability $c_m(\varepsilon)$. Under the assumption of independence, this probability will be the product of the individual probabilities for each pair. That is, if the observations are independent,

$$c_m(\varepsilon) = c_1^m(\varepsilon)$$

To estimate the probability for a particular dimension, it is necessary to go through all the possible sets of that length that can be drawn from the sample and count the number of sets which satisfy the epsilon condition. The ratio of the number of sets satisfying the condition divided by the total number of sets provides the estimate of the probability. Given a sample of n observations of a series X, the condition will be:

$$c_{m,n}(\varepsilon) = \frac{2}{(n-m+1)(n-m)} \sum_{s=1}^{n-m+1} \sum_{t=s+1}^{n-m+1} \prod_{j=0}^{m-1} I_\varepsilon(X_{s+j} X_{t+j}) \tag{4.1}$$

where $I\varepsilon$ is the indicator function:

$$\begin{aligned} I_\varepsilon(x, y) &= 1, if |x - y| \leq \varepsilon \\ &= 0 \text{ otherwise} \end{aligned} \tag{4.2}$$

The statistics $c_{m,n}(\varepsilon)$ are often referred to as correlation integrals. These sample estimates of the probabilities can be used to construct a test statistic for independence:

Table 4.1 Test for non-linearity of the stock indices (BDS statistic)

	Dimension				
Market	2	3	4	5	6
Argentina	0.017711*	0.040876*	0.058331*	0.068361*	0.071993*
Australia	0.023558*	0.047349*	0.06565*	0.076892*	0.082518*
Austria	0.029364*	0.060486*	0.083314*	0.097237*	0.10341*
Belgium	0.03103*	0.061446*	0.08671*	0.103583*	0.112641*
Brazil	0.017188*	0.032977*	0.046445*	0.054426*	0.05827*
Cairo	0.03991*	0.078498*	0.104148*	0.121957*	0.13287*
Canada	0.021196*	0.04589*	0.066192*	0.079857*	0.086206*
China	0.014301*	0.033863*	0.050445*	0.060513*	0.065851*
DJ30	0.0176*	0.03932*	0.056384*	0.068244*	0.074805*
France	0.01562*	0.03616*	0.053553*	0.064993*	0.071044*
Germany	0.017714*	0.043838*	0.064495*	0.077191*	0.084745*
Hong Kong	0.015304*	0.035771*	0.054732*	0.067487*	0.074046*
India	0.023633*	0.04658*	0.064677*	0.07604*	0.082239*
Indonesia	0.023774*	0.047617*	0.064276*	0.072759*	0.074592*
Japan	0.009672*	0.022691*	0.032983*	0.039199*	0.043124*
Malaysia	0.038397*	0.077432*	0.103973*	0.119009*	0.124461*
Mexico	0.018527*	0.038931*	0.055712*	0.066456*	0.072675*
NASDAQ	0.022024*	0.05154*	0.073855*	0.090437*	0.100938*
Netherlands	0.025049*	0.054301*	0.078862*	0.094762*	0.103678*
New Zealand	0.023984*	0.048088*	0.063819*	0.071304*	0.073555*
Norway	0.027221*	0.053404*	0.072898*	0.08281*	0.086514*
Seoul	0.014173*	0.036808*	0.056005*	0.07034*	0.07995*
Singapore	0.021381*	0.047456*	0.069255*	0.081906*	0.088407*
S&P500	0.016842*	0.039202*	0.057046*	0.070369*	0.078091*
Spain	0.018697*	0.03886*	0.054231*	0.066653*	0.073445*
Stockholm	0.018892*	0.043379*	0.063321*	0.077026*	0.084125*
Switzerland	0.025369*	0.052118*	0.073939*	0.087112*	0.093795*
Taiwan	0.009362*	0.026554*	0.042726*	0.054021*	0.06091*
Tel Aviv	0.01015*	0.023353*	0.033066*	0.039107*	0.042958*
UK	0.020569*	0.043737*	0.063342*	0.076746*	0.084373*

*: significant at 1% level of significance

$$b_{m,n}(\varepsilon) = c_{m,n}(\varepsilon) - c_{1,n-m+1}(\varepsilon) \tag{4.3}$$

The second term discards the last $m-1$ observations from the sample so that it is based on the same number of terms as the first statistic. Under the assumption of independence, this statistic could be close to zero.

The result of BDS test is summarized in Table 4.1.

All thirty stock indices, as can be seen from the table, are significantly nonlinear. The rejection of the null of IID by the BDS statistic, although provides evidence of the series being nonlinear, it does not necessarily mean the time series exhibits chaotic behavior. Rejection of IID can be consistent with any of the following four types of non-IID behavior: linear dependence, non-stationarity, nonlinear stochastic processes and nonlinear deterministic process (chaos).

Since all stock indices are non-stationary, only linear dependence should be removed by suitable filtering before proceeding further to discriminate between nonlinearities due to stochastic behavior and nonlinearities due to the existence of chaotic behavior. All indices are characterized by significant autocorrelation and hence need to be AR filtered. Otherwise the data will be less reliable while applied to a nonlinear model. Order of AR has been determined by minimum AIC criterion. This non-linearity however, can be generated from a stochastic (ARCH type) model or from chaotic behavior. To remove that, the AR filtered series are filtered again by a suitable GARCH model.

The appropriate series are passed through the following tests to find out any possible presence of chaos. The study follows the methodology proposed by Kodba et al. (2004) for possible chaotic behavior of a driven resonant circuit and further by Perc for presence of determinism in human electrocardiogram (2005a) and in human locomotory system (2005b). The following section tries to replicate that for financial market data. The methodology as proposed by Kodba et al. (2004) is restated and explained in the following sections before going into the result and its explanation. The same methodology has been used by Chakrabarti et al. (2010) and Sen et al. (2011) in the context of foreign exchange markets.

4.2.2 The State-Space Reconstruction

The first problem faced while studying deterministic properties of a time series model is that the data available is not a phase space object. Before starting the discussion regarding detection of chaos, it is necessary to explain what a phase space or state space (these two terms are often used interchangeably) is. A phase space is a collection of possible system states. A system state at any point contains all information needed to determine the future states. It is necessary to know the phase space in order to model the system. However, the phase space is often unknown. Therefore it is necessary to reconstruct the phase space to be able to develop a model.

The data, here, the stock indices data is a series of scalars. So, the state-space reconstruction of the data into state vectors is required (Kantz and Schreiber 2004). The reconstructed attractor or trajectory of the original system is given by, according to Taken's (1981) embedding theorem

$$p(i) = \left(x_i, x_{i+\tau}, x_{i+2\tau}, \ldots, x_{i+(m-1)\tau}\right) \tag{4.4}$$

where τ is time delay parameter and m is the embedding dimension. τ is the time difference between adjacent components of p(i). The idea of a state space reconstruction is to replace every state variable with a delayed variable of it. The reconstructed vector of the delayed variables has the same intrinsic characteristics as the original state variables, like the trajectory, Lyapunov exponent, etc. given the embedding dimension m is large enough. The advantage of the state space reconstruction is that it can deal with a large dimension and yet can be noise free.

A proper choice of τ and m is equally important. τ should be large enough so as to make the set of information containing in x_i and $x_{\tau+i}$ to be significantly different i.e. all the trajectories will seem to lie on the same line. Again if the chosen τ is too large, the system will hardly retain its memory of the initial states.

4.2.3 Mutual Information Criterion: Finding τ

The mutual information criteria (MIC) (Fraser and Sweeney 1986) can effectively calculate the optimum τ. The criterion shows the general dependence between two variables. It is the information available about the state $x_{i+\tau}$ given x_i.

In calculation of the MIC, observations are arranged in ascending order and then are divided in h equal intervals. The MIC is given as follows:

$$I(\tau) = -\sum_{h=1}^{j}\sum_{k=1}^{j} P_{h,k}(\tau) ln \frac{P_{h,k}(\tau)}{P_h P_k} \quad (4.5)$$

where P_h is the probability that the variable falls into the interval h

P_k is the probability that the variable falls into the interval k

$P_{h,k}(\tau)$ is the joint probability of one variable falls into the interval h and another falls into the interval $h + \tau$, τ being the time delay.

The procedure offers an optimum τ incase the appropriate probability density function is known. MIC's ability to capture nonlinear correlation makes it score over the autocorrelation technique.

The optimum time delay is the τ where $I(\tau)$ hits its first minima. Because, in a system with chaotic dynamics, as $\tau \to \infty$, $I(\tau) \to 0$ as the correlation between x_h and x_k becomes negligible. At the first minima, $x_{i+\tau}$ adds the most to the available information from x_i without losing the correlation between them completely.

Now the appropriate embedding dimension has to be determined.

4.2.4 False Nearest Neighborhood: Decide the Optimal m

This study uses the technique of False Nearest Neighborhood (FNN) to estimate the appropriate embedding dimension. This method was proposed by Kennel et al. (1992). The concept is that for an optimum embedding dimension m, the reconstructed delay space is topologically consistent with the original state space. Therefore, two points in the neighborhood, when subjected to a short forward iteration, continues to be in the neighborhood. If, a point i has a neighbor j that after a forward iteration does not remain in the neighborhood of i anymore, j is said to be a false nearest neighbor of i. When the reconstructed delay space is formed with too small embedding dimensions, the reconstructed space ceases to be topologically consistent with the original state space and points after forward iteration may appear to be in the neighborhood while actually they are far apart.

Let *p*(*i*) be a point on a m-dimensional reconstructed space with a nearest neighbor *p*(*j*). If *d* be the Euclidean distance between two points, defined as

$$d(m) = ||x_i(m) - x_j(m)|| \tag{4.6}$$

Then, for nearest neighbors, the distance *d* is minimized. Now, the next objective is to iterate for a bigger dimension and check whether *d* is still minimized. The embedding dimension is increased by one so that

$$d(m+1) = ||x_i(m+1) - x_j(m+1)|| \tag{4.7}$$

If *p*(*i*) is a false nearest neighbor of *p*(*j*) then *d*(*m* + *1*) will not be minimized. This is characterized by the change of distance between the two points with the embedding dimension increased from *d* to *d* + *1* being larger than an acceptable tolerance level. This can be expressed as

$$\frac{|x_{i+m\tau} - x_{j+m\tau}|}{d(m)} > R_t \tag{4.8}$$

where R_t is distance ratio threshold. The value of the *m* will be chosen in such a manner for which the percentage of false nearest neighbors in the dataset falls to zero.

The choice of R_t, although subjective in nature, has to be made carefully (Rhodes and Morari 1997). For a R_t that is too small will not result the FNN to drop to zero at the correct embedding dimension. On the other hand, a R_t that is too large tends to accept a lower embedding dimension than what actually should be.

According to Kennel et al. (1992), for most cases $R_t = 10$ proves to be a good choice.

Lastly, although the FNN is a widely used process, it is still not robust in the presence of noise.

4.2.5 Determinism Test

In the next section of the study the underlying series are tested for determinism. That is whether the truly chaotic or a random one which apparently looks like chaotic. Kaplan and Glass (1992) proposed an effective technique to check whether the series is truly deterministic. In our study we shall be using exactly the same technique. But before we proceed, let us see how the idea is developed.

To start with, the attractor is plotted in a *x*(*t*) vs. *x*(*t*-τ) space. The phase space is grained into $q \times q$ grids so that each grid has a part of the attractor passing through it. A directional vector of unit length is assigned to each grid that corresponds to the portion of attractor in it. This vector is called the trajectory vector. If e_i be the unit vector passing through each box, then the resultant vector V_k from all the vector passes is just a simple average given by

$$V_k = \frac{1}{P_k}\sum_{i=1}^{P_k} e_i \tag{4.9}$$

where P_k is the number of passes through the kth grid.

Now for a deterministic system, the phase space offers a unique solution. For that, the unit vectors in a grid must follow the same direction, that is, the trajectories inside the grid must never cross, whereas for a stochastic system the trajectories inside the grid cross each other. As the crossing never occurs in deterministic system, V_k is of unit length and for stochastic system, value of V_k is significantly lower than one.

4.2.6 Maximum Lyapunov Exponent

Lyapunov exponent (Λ) measures the degree of separation between infinitesimally close trajectories in phase space. For a chaotic system, the trajectories diverge continuously as the system is dependent on initial conditions. For a m-dimensional system, there are m numbers of Lyapunov exponents. Of this spectrum of Lyapunov exponents, most important is the maximum Lyapunov exponent ($\Lambda_{\max}$) which is an indicator of chaos. For $\Lambda_{\max} > 0$, the system is chaotic and close trajectories diverge in phase space.

The calculation of the $\Lambda_{\max}$ as proposed by Wolf et al. (1985) involves the following steps. First, an initial point $p(0)$ is chosen with a nearest neighbor. The distance between them be L_0. Now the points are iterated toward by time t_{evolv} (which is essentially equal to τ) and the distance after iteration is noted (L_{evolv}). If the system is chaotic, the trajectories diverge in time and hence $L_{evolv} > L_0$. The value of t_{evolv} has to be less than $m\tau$, a larger value will result in an underestimation of $\Lambda_{\max}$. At the end of first iteration, a replacement is made to choose a new nearest neighbor for the evolved $p(0)$. This process has to continue till $p(0)$ reaches the end of the series. Maximum Lyapunov exponent can be presented as:

$$\Lambda_{max} = \frac{1}{Mt_{evolv}}\sum_{i=0}^{M} ln\frac{L_{evolv}^{(i)}}{L_0^{(i)}} \tag{4.10}$$

With the understanding of the methodology, the next section tabulates and explains the results obtained from the above tests.

4.3 Results

The study explores the possible presence of chaos in the global market in two phases. The study considers the nature of the global stock markets during the two stock market cycles chosen in the study. Hence, the first phase considers the first

Table 4.2 Detection of possible chaos in stock indices (phase 1)

	Emb delay	Shannon entropy	Embed dimension	Determinism	Lyapmax
Argentina	1	3.257	5	0.8637	0.1956
Australia	2	3.342	5	0.703	0.0525
Austria	1	4	5	0.8489	0.2149
Belgium	4	2.275	4	0.6558	0.4775
Brazil	2	2.715	5	0.6402	0.2793
Cairo	1	2.697	4	0.8009	0.1307
Canada	1	3.215	4	0.8336	−0.8623
China	1	3.201	5	0.8641	0.0807
DJ30	1	2.042	5	0.7945	−0.0417
France	1	3.595	5	0.8743	0.08
Germany	1	2.495	4	0.89	−0.01
Hong Kong	1	3.138	5	0.859	−0.3167
India	2	3.335	5	0.7325	2633
Indonesia	2	3.123	4	0.7505	0.0433
Japan	1	3.604	5	0.8708	−0.1629
Malaysia	1	2.112	5	0.7595	−0.1315
Mexico	1	3.099	5	0.8167	0.7431
NASDAQ	1	3.367	5	0.8363	0.335
Netherlands	2	3.411	5	0.681	0.6167
New Zealand	3	4.005	3	0.6335	−0.9357
Norway	2	3.66	4	0.6991	−0.177
Seoul	1	3.544	5	0.8635	0.1689
Singapore	1	3.038	5	0.8226	−0.403
S&P500	1	3.534	4	0.875	0.261
Spain	NA	NA	NA	NA	NA
Stockholm	1	3.374	5	0.8674	0.227
Switzerland	2	3.509	5	0.6635	−1.6719
Taiwan	1	3.476	4	0.8883	0.3097
Tel Aviv	1	3.238	5	0.8756	0.7715
UK	1	3.617	4	0.8691	0.1738

stock market cycle and is extended over the period of 1998–2005. The second phase covers the second cycle and considers the period from 2006 to 2011. The results are tabulated in the Tables 4.2 and 4.3.

Table 4.2 summarizes the results for phase 1 (1998–2005). The exercise could not be performed for the Spanish market due to lack of availability of data. The remaining twenty nine series are found to be deterministic. However, not all of them are chaotic. Out of theses twenty nine markets, ten are found to be non-chaotic. These include three European markets (namely, Switzerland, Germany and Norway), five Asia–Pacific markets (namely, New Zealand, Singapore, Hong Kong, Japan and Malaysia), and two American markets (namely Dow Jones 30 and Canada).

Table 4.3 summarizes the results for phase 2. The determinism factors for all the indices are quite high. However, out of the thirty stock indices the Maximum Lyapunov exponent has been non-positive for only six of them. Therefore, the

Table 4.3 Detection of possible chaos in stock indices (phase 2)

	Emb delay	Shannon entropy	Embed. dim.	Determinism	Lyapmax
Hong Kong	1	3.066	5	0.8484	−0.5089
New Zealand	4	3.266	4	0.6989	−0.4826
Tel Aviv	1	3.2	5	0.7802	−0.4055
UK	1	3.191	5	0.8556	−0.223
Cairo	1	2.042	5	0.7945	−0.0447
Malaysia	2	1.824	5	0.1177	−0.0005
Argentina	1	3.329	5	0.8596	0.2265
Germany	1	3.394	5	0.873248	0.2444
Norway	1	3.501	4	0.8621	0.2809
Canada	2	3.133	5	0.7214	0.3005
India	1	3.095	4	0.8586	0.3364
Taiwan	1	3.591	5	0.8496	0.3823
Australia	1	3.459	5	0.8496	0.3936
Netherlands	1	3.201	5	0.8394	0.4131
Singapore	1	3.332	5	0.8422	0.445
S&P500	1	3.024	5	0.8323	0.4592
DJ30	1	3.026	4	0.861	0.5097
Belgium	2	3.302	5	0.679	0.5137
China	1	3.577	5	0.8685	0.5378
Indonesia	4	3.368	5	0.7066	0.5866
Mexico	1	3.351	5	0.8543	0.6424
Brazil	1	3.236	5	0.8468	0.6857
Japan	1	3.095	5	0.8359	0.6877
Austria	1	3.362	5	0.8487	0.7149
Spain	1	3.099	5	0.8166	0.7431
France	1	3.232	5	0.8383	0.7577
Stockholm	1	3.471	5	0.8511	0.9291
Seoul	1	3.103	5	0.8289	1.0224
Switzerland	1	3.062	5	0.858	1.2426
NASDAQ	1	3.17	5	0.8574	2.572

remaining twenty four markets are chaotic in nature. Specifically, all the US and American indexes are chaotic. Within the Asia–Pacific region, stock markets of Hong Kong, New Zealand and Malaysia are only deterministic. All the European markets except for UK are chaotic. The two middle-east markets of Cairo and Tel Aviv are found to be non-chaotic.

The nature of markets during the two phases thus has some points in common. Over the different stock market cycles, the stock markets are always deterministic, if not chaotic. However, while over the first cycle nineteen markets were found to be chaotic, the number increases to twenty four during the second phase of the study. The markets of Hong Kong, New Zealand and Malaysia have never been chaotic over the study period.

These findings have significant investment as well as policy significance. But before analyzing that, let us summarize the findings of the study.

4.4 The Dynamics of Global Stock Market: The Emerging Issues

The empirical study of global market crashes has produced results significant for the individual investors as well as the policy makers. Over a period of thirteen years running from 1998 to 2011, the world market has experienced two significant stock market cycles that have been the foci of this study. The first cycle was around the so-called Internet Bubble of late twentieth and early twenty first century. The second one is related to the more recent financial crisis that has often been referred to as the worst since the Great Depression of 1930s.

Out of these two prominent cycles, the second cycle, rather than the first one has been more general in nature affecting all the thirty markets considered in the study. The study has uncovered significant latent structure in the global stock market over these two cycles. The nature of such structure differs significantly from one cycle to another. During the first cycle, the market was dominated by a single trend where the European and the American markets remained the significant players in the sense that these markets explained significant portion of total variation in global stock market returns. These two regions have been closely associated and completely decoupled from the Asian markets. The US markets, however, were not characterized by any lead-lag relationship among them. The second cycle has been characterized by three distinct structures. The European markets emerged as the dominant group in the global market followed by the Asian markets. The American markets, on the contrary, have lost their dominance. The three regions, however, are completely dissociated from each other. The European and the American regions have been mostly characterized by an absence of strong lead-lag relationship. The presence of intra-regional association, however, has been stronger in the Asian region. The European markets thus, over the years, have remained the epicenter of financial crises. The Asian region, however, was the safest during the first cycle and not so risky during the second one. The findings have significant implication for global investors. Investors could reap maximum advantage of global portfolio diversification by investing in non-associated markets. The non-association of three significant regions offers immense scope for inter-regional portfolio diversification at the global level. The Asian market perhaps has remained the proper place for investment. There are however, opportunities for intra-regional diversifications even in the recent period of recovery. This is evident from the non-association of markets within a given region. There is however, still some warning of market instability in the sense that the market is still dominated by a single trend. While the first boom was a real bull period; the recent recovery is yet to be considered as a period of strong market growth.

The variability transmission mechanism during the stock market cycles has a particular feature. The variability in a particular market can hardly be attributed to the variability of the other markets with which it is associated. This is particularly the point that made us probe into the possible chaotic nature of the global stock market. We found the global stock market to be mostly deterministic and in some cases, chaotic. The markets will thus be characterized by non-periodic cycles and trends where volatility and fluctuations generate endogenously. These make global stock markets inherently unstable, or they could at best be described by knife-edge stability. Cycles and crashes are manifestations of this inherent instability: norms rather than aberrations. There is no determinate equilibrium and no external shock will be required to gear financial crisis at regular intervals which, in an integrated financial world, will reverberate across the globe in no time.

The fact that the global stock markets are indeed chaotic or at least deterministic in nature has significant theoretical and policy implications. An initial infinitesimally small change in an index can have a major impact on the future and as the time glides, economic forecasts become less reliable. The relevant equations of motion underlying the global stock market return, no doubt can be determined, but it would be nearly impossible to forecast beyond a short time frame. For the global stock markets, instability will be intrinsic rather than aberration. Policy prescriptions, based on the presumption of linearity are likely to be ineffective when applied on a system which is actually nonlinear. The findings have significant bearing at the theoretical level too. A chaotic stock market invalidates the assumption of efficient market. With efficient market hypothesis on trial, some investment strategies that were discarded earlier will now appear to be lucrative and effective. Strategies involving market timing, value investing and tactical asset allocation could be profitable and now investors can very well capitalize on market cycles. In a chaotic or at least deterministic global stock market the traditional asset pricing models to analyze stock price movements are required to be reframed. It is so because, a deterministic series invalidates the Gaussian assumption about probability distribution on which traditional methods of market analysis rest. Moreover, the traditional models cannot incorporate infinite variance property of such fractal distributions and are based on static mean reversion. These provide further basis for reformulation of traditional asset pricing models. The market analysts while explaining market movements, should act cautiously as the traditional econometric techniques often cannot capture the irregular cycles of a chaotic market. However, even with a dynamic quantitative technique, it would be unwise to predict future movements because long-term economic forecasting is no longer feasible.

References

Baranger N (2001) Chaos, complexity and entropy: a physics talk for non physicists. Wesleyan University Physics Department Colloquium. http://www.necsi.org/projects/baranger/cce.html. Accessed 14 March 2011

Barnett WA, Gallant AR, Hinich MJ, Jungeilges J, Kaplan D, Jensen MJ (1997) A single-blind controlled competition among tests for non-linearity and chaos. J Econometrics 82:157–192

Brock WA, Hsieh DA, LeBaron B (1991) Nonlinear dynamics, chaos and instability: statistical theory and economic evidence. MIT Press, Cambridge

Brock WA, Dechert W, Scheinkman J (1996) A test for independence based on the correlation dimension. Economet Rev 15(3):197–235

Chakrabarti G (2010a) Dynamics of global stock market: crisis and beyond. Vdm-Verlag, Germany

Chakrabarti G (2010b) Propagator of global stock market volatility in recent years: Asian versus non-Asian markets. Empirical Econ Lett 9(4):397–403

Chakrabarti G, Sen C, Sarkar A (2010) Spot-forward rate relationship revisited: an analysis in the light of non-linearity and chaos. J Int Econ 1(2):73–87

Fraser AM, Swinney HL (1986) Independent coordinates for strange attractors from mutual information. Phys Rev A 33:1134–1140

Grassberger P, Procaccia I (1983) Measuring the strangeness of strange attractors. Phys D: Nonlinear Phenom 9(1–2):189–208

Hadamard JS (1898) Les surfaces à courbures opposées et leurs lignes géodésiques. J Math Pures et Appl 4:27–73

Kantz H, Schreiber T (2004) Dimension estimates and physiological data. Chaos 5:143–154

Kaplan DT, Glass L (1992) Direct test for determinism in a time series. Phys Rev Lett 68:427–430

Kennel MB, Brown R, Abarbanel HDI (1992) Determining embedding dimension for phase space reconstruction using a geometrical construction. Phys Rev A 45:3403–3411

Kodba S, Perc M, Marhl M (2004) Detecting chaos from a time series. Eur J Phys 26:205–215

Perc M (2005a) Nonlinear time series analysis of the human electrocardiogram. Eur J Phys 26:757–768

Perc M (2005b) The dynamics of human gait. Eur J Phys 26:525–534

Rhodes C, Morari M (1997) The false nearest neighbors algorithm: an overview. Comput Chem Eng 2(1):S1149–S1154

Sen C, Chakrabarti G, Sarkar A (2011) Evidence of chaos: a tale of two exchange rates. Empirical Econ Lett 10(8):777–784

Stewart I (2002) Does god play dice? the new mathematics of chaos, 2nd edn. Blackwell Publishers Inc, Malden

Takens F (1981) Detecting strange attractor in turbulence. In: Rand DA, Young LS (eds) Lecture notes in mathematics. Springer, Berlin

Theiler J (1986) Spurious dimension from correlation algorithms applied to limited time series data. Phys Rev A 34(3):2427–2432

Wolf A, Swift JB, Swinney HL, Vastano JA (1985) Determining Lyapunov exponents from a time series. Physica D 16:285–317

MIX
Papier aus verantwortungsvollen Quellen
Paper from responsible sources
FSC® C105338
FSC
www.fsc.org

If you have any concerns about our products,
you can contact us on
ProductSafety@springernature.com

In case Publisher is established outside the EU,
the EU authorized representative is:
Springer Nature Customer Service Center GmbH
Europaplatz 3, 69115 Heidelberg, Germany

Printed by Libri Plureos GmbH
in Hamburg, Germany